NOBODY'S CHILDREN
The Foster Care Crisis in Canada

NOBODY'S CHILDREN
The Foster Care Crisis in Canada

Martyn Kendrick

MACMILLAN OF CANADA
A Division of Canada Publishing Corporation
Toronto, Ontario, Canada

Canadian Cataloguing in Publication Data

Kendrick, Martyn, 1953–
　Nobody's Children

Includes bibliographical references.
ISBN 0–7715–9207–8

1. Foster home care — Canada.　2. Child welfare — Canada.　3. Family policy — Canada.　I. Title.

HV887.C3K46 1990　　362.7'33'0971　　C90–093022–5

1　2　3　4　5　　　ARC　94　93　92　91　90

Jacket and text design: Robert MacDonald/Media Clones

MACMILLAN OF CANADA
A Division of Canada Publishing Corporation
Toronto, Ontario, Canada

Printed & Bound in Canada by Friesen Printers

Typeset by Colborne, Cox & Burns Typographers Inc.

CONTENTS

ACKNOWLEDGMENTS

Writing a book is a solitary project, although many people contribute to the final product. John Meston, Fay Martin, many young people in care, and countless youth on the street aided my understanding of the issues. I hope I have done justice to their concerns.

Sheldon Fischer, my editor, is responsible in more ways than I can say for whatever is said well here. He encouraged, probed, prodded, added insight, and, above all, believed that the intangible line of argument I was pursuing was still there during those periods when I had lost sight of it.

Without the generous assistance of the Canada Council I could not have completed the work, and for that I am grateful.

As always, my agent, Larry Hoffman, has encouraged me in his inimitable way and kept me on track, while my wife, Lucille, and our daughter, Justine, have balanced out the life.

Martyn Kendrick
Hamilton
November 1989

For my father,
and for all the Richard Cardinals
who sink beneath our wisdom like stones.

PREFACE

Yes, there was a lot of kids there that was sexually and physically abused. Lots of them. It was hard. But if you are asking, sir, if they should close it down, no. Absolutely not, 'cause what they'd do is just take all the kids in there and stuff them in foster homes. And that's worse. I've been there. I know.
     Derek O'Brien, former foster child and resident of St. John's Mount Cashel orphanage, speaking with CBC's Michael Enright, November 30, 1989

The greatest terror a child can have is that he is not loved, and rejection is the hell he fears. And with rejection comes anger, and with anger some kind of crime in revenge for the rejection, and with the crime guilt — and there is the story of mankind.
     John Steinbeck, *East of Eden*

As recently as ten years ago society remained generally silent about the phenomenon of child abuse. No longer. We are daily barraged by reports in the media that children are brutally maltreated by their parents, the very people who should be giving them the most protection. Children are beaten until their bodies no longer heal, they are scalded in pots of boiling water, locked in basement kennels, starved until their skin shrivels, and forced to perform acts so depraved we

can barely entertain the thought of them. If not physically mis-
treated, they are verbally assaulted, emotionally deprived, sometimes abandoned.

We rush to protect such children, and rightly so. As good citizens,
as parents and humanitarians, we expect "someone" to do "something" about it. But who are those "someones" who should be
acting to prevent abuse? And what does "protection" mean? What
actually happens to children who are removed from their homes and
become crown wards dependent on the state?

During the last two years, the people of Saskatchewan have been
reeling under the revelations of former inmates of Bosco's Children's
Homes who accused the Catholic priests and lay staff of having
physically and emotionally abused them for years. The provincial
child protection agencies had for decades been unwittingly placing
abandoned children in these homes. This same tragic scenario
played itself out in Newfoundland's Mount Cashel orphanage,
where investigations continued into 1990. Thousands of group and
foster homes, residential treatment centres, and orphanages in
North America house, at last count, more than 200,000 abused,
abandoned, and neglected children. Are these two sensational cases
an anomaly among them?

Each year Canada's child protection and family service agencies
intervene in the lives of tens of thousands of Canadian families. The
public assumes rather blithely that when children are removed from an
allegedly abusive environment, it is guaranteed that they will be placed
in a better one. This is a comforting but naive belief. Each year the
crisis-driven authorities of the Canadian child protection agencies gam-
ble the fate of thousands of children on an uncertain, fragmented,
bureaucratic, and failing system. Although the experiences the children
suffer are not always as extreme as in the Bosco and Mount Cashel
affairs, the root problems faced by a majority of children in state care
are the same ones as gave rise to those distressing cases.

Children in care anywhere outside their natural homes will have
most areas of their life regularly mishandled. They will be placed
inappropriately. They will be moved from one home to another.
They will depend upon untrained, underpaid, and frustrated foster
parents or group home workers who become their primary care

givers. They will experience infrequent visits from social workers and psychologists, condescension and secretiveness about their cases, and haphazard methods of case planning. If they are made permanent crown wards — that is, if parental rights are terminated — they will become solely dependent on the state and its harried, overworked representatives.

At last, at the end of their transit through the system, they will be thrust at 16 or 18, with little or no preparation, into an unwelcoming world. Still suffering the psychological consequences of alienation and abuse in their pre- and post-care surroundings, they will enter society grossly undereducated, unskilled and therefore unemployable, and confused, lonely, frustrated, and angry. Adolescents with these characteristics are destined for menial labour or welfare and are predisposed towards mental-health problems, suicide, homelessness, delinquency, and ultimately, prison. Many of the graduates of foster and group home care end up on the streets.

I have chosen in this book to highlight problems and contradictions specifically of the foster care system because it serves as a window into the fractured world of child protection. Through it, we can see clearly the assumptions that guide the decision-making processes of a wide range of child protection services and can envision what it means to live as an abandoned or abused child within the context of the sprawling network of governmental or quasi-governmental organizations.

Next to adoption, foster care is considered by child advocates the best solution the state has to offer those children whose parents were perceived to have failed them. (However, the older children now coming into care are difficult to place out for adoption.) Group and residential homes, treatment centres, and training and reform schools are, in descending order, the placements of least preference. If the foster home fails, the children and adolescents in care are cast adrift in this system, moving from their parental home to a foster home to a group home to a residential treatment centre to a training school — from caring to caretaking to controlling.

Although crown wards living in Canadian foster homes represent only a fraction of the disturbed youth who are served by the various arms of the child protection industry, it is important to understand how this particular arm of the industry works: if the best form of treatment and intervention we have fails these youths — the most promising and least blameworthy to come under the authority of the child protection agencies — it follows that lesser forms of treatment/intervention will fail even more drastically.

As in most areas of child protection, there is a crisis in foster care today: a chronic shortage of homes and skilled surrogate parents. Critics despair that this signals the end of this preferred form of placement. I do not see the demise of foster care as a reason for despair. Foster care, despite its misguided champions, has historically been a way for government to get child welfare "on the cheap," as one astute critic put it back in 1927. I look at the crisis as an unfortunate but very timely impetus and as an opportunity to re-examine the roots of a system that has been failing for a century.

At a recent child care conference in Chicago, John Wodarski, professor and director of research into adolescent behaviour at the University of Georgia, argued that "the empirical data to support the effectiveness of therapeutic services to children and adolescents indicate no substantial improvement, and even more disheartening, deterioration in many instance." Perhaps it's time, he suggested, "that we re-examined our basic assumptions."[1]

This unsettling conclusion comes at a time when there is a high incidence of emotional disturbance, drug and alcohol abuse, suicide, delinquency, gross underachievement, and random violence among adolescents. It comes at a time when we deploy more money and human resources than ever before on prevention and rehabilitation programs aimed at troubled youth. It comes at a time when more and more children are being removed from their homes and placed under the authority of, and treated by, child protection agents.

Over the next five years, because of mounting public awareness and increased reporting of physical and sexual abuse, and because of mandatory reporting laws for professionals, anonymous public hotlines, increased immigration, and the trend towards deinstitutionalization of all but the most severely mentally and physically handicapped, an increasing number of young people will be placed under the authority of child protection agencies. For their sake it is time to re-examine some of our basic assumptions.

Most books on Canadian child welfare offer numbers and statistics couched in the jargon of various bureaucracies or disciplines. They are written by academics, ministry-appointed commissions, psychologists, social scientists, and consultants to any one of the above. Rarely do the children and adolescents they serve come to life in these pages. The writers describe an abstract phenomenon from the perspective of adults prescribing treatments, almost like a doctor dispensing pills over the phone. I have tried to give a face to this indiscriminate mass of troubled youth. I have attempted as often as possible to describe the system and its impacts on the emotional stability of young people in care. I let them speak about the system as it affects their lives because for centuries their voice has been silenced — which may explain in part why most of society's benevolent attempts have failed.

And I have written out of personal experience, deeply felt, and painfully recalled.

The book is in two parts. The first six chapters describe the system in some detail and deal with the historical development and underlying assumptions of child protection. The last three chapters explore current trends and isolated movements within the system that lend hope to an otherwise dismal picture.

Although many critical comments are made throughout the text, I do not want to be misunderstood. Most of the people who work in child welfare are well intentioned. They bring to their work enthusiasm, compassion, and high ideals. But the bureaucratic system they work within has a way of dampening energy, misdirecting compassion, and deflating idealism. It is the system that needs to be changed if the talents of these people are to be used effectively in the service of children and families. It is my hope that this appeal on behalf of dependent youth complements the efforts both of the young people themselves and of frustrated adults within the system who want to help them to transform what is now a barren system into a nurturing environment.

1

CRISIS

I was six when I first got put in care. My mom left and my dad couldn't do anything I guess and so he put me in there [Ontario Children's Aid Society]. I went with five families. I don't remember much. I heard I went to five when they were discussing my case once when I was at the case conference. I just remember going to different places. When I was 10 I ran away. My dad would write me and visit sometimes so I knew where he was, and I went back to him. I never saw my mom. He said I could stay with him at first. He was drinking a lot. I stayed with him until I was 12, maybe 13, and then I got sent to another foster home 'cause I wasn't going to school all the time and stuff. I went to two places in a year.

The first one the woman was nice but the guy was loco. He was an ex-cop or OPP [Ontario Provincial Police officer] and he'd beat up me and the other guy that was there, for nothing . . . all the time. We had to be in at 6:30 every night and we stayed in. He was pretty strict. I took off and he caught me and beat me black and blue, then phoned the Aid and said I was too much trouble. He said I got in a fight outside. I told the social worker before that that I wanted to get out of there and so I didn't care. I was lucky [laughs]. The other guy had to stay there.

The next home was really good. They was really nice.

They got along real good with me. But then one day the social worker came and told them that they had found something for me they thought was okay. I didn't want to go and they told her that they liked me but she said it was done. I didn't know her [social worker]. She was different than the last one, so I was pretty pissed off. I took off from there too. When I got caught they sent me to the Sally Anne home in London [Ontario]. That wasn't bad. There was six cottages and some of us stayed in one and some in another. I was in Cottage Six and he [male house parent] was always finding reasons to brick us. He used to want to box us. He'd been in the army and we couldn't and so he'd take us aside and say okay let's go, and then he'd start beating on us. We didn't do anything. He said it would make us tough. We had to call him Uncle. I told my social worker about him and he said it wasn't true.

There was a girl I liked in Cottage One and she was getting it [sexual abuse] from the Uncle there. The Aunt [female house parent] didn't know. She told her social worker too, but nothing happened. So we ran away. I must have been there about a year. When they caught us they said we could stay if we were better. I said that we was getting beaten and abused sexually, not me, but my girlfriend, and they said that I was making it up. I said that it wasn't me that needed to be better but them. I just wanted to stay someplace and have friends and stuff. So I left there and went back home.

My dad said as long as I was good I could stay, but he was never there so I just did what I wanted. They made me go to psychiatrists and stuff and they sent me to a vocational school. I hated it. They asked me what I wanted to do and I didn't know. I don't know what I want now, for Christ's sake. I started skipping school and would steal cars and stuff and they sent me to court and the judge said I needed to learn a lesson and he sent me to Guelph Reform School. I had just turned 16. That place was scary. There was guys in there who'd knife ya while they're smilin' at ya. One guy, big guy in there, was playing cards and he liked me, and one of the other guys was looking at my cards and I said, "Hey, stop looking at my cards, that's cheating." Just like that. I didn't mean nothing. And this other big guy that likes me, he just hauled off and let him have it. He kept hittin' him. And he says, "You don't do that around here." Later I said to the guy he hit, "I'm sorry, I didn't mean it." And he said it was okay. That's the kind of people you got to deal with in there.

They sent me to Brampton Training School after one month. You didn't have to stay in a cell and there were no fences and stuff. They were all guys in there and we went to school and worked in the shop and did sports. It wasn't bad. It was open, and if you were okay you got out early and got to go home or whatever. If you tried to run, you were sent back to Guelph. I got out of there when I was near 18. That was eight years ago and I haven't been in a lot of trouble since.

[He was asked to comment on school and friends.] I had a couple of girlfriends, like the girl in London [does not remember her name] and one girl I knocked up. I said I would help with the baby, but she didn't want it and she got an abortion and I couldn't see that so I just said, I'm off, just like that, 'cause I don't believe in that stuff. I'm seeing a girl now, just friends, but I like her. She thinks I should take a course, maybe an apprenticeship with somebody and get some work I like. I only got grade 10. I worked up in the camps [Northern Ontario logging camps] for a summer. You can make a lot of money up there. But you gotta be careful. Lot of guys just want to rip you off. Not the bosses, the guys working in the camp. Anyway, I'm here now [Hamilton] and I'm gonna keep this job [gas station attendant] for as long as I can. He's [gas station owner] pretty square with me. I like my place, I guess. It's mine anyway [a rooming house in Hamilton's heavily industrialized east end]. But I don't know. My dad died two years ago so there's not much for me here, is there?[1]

In 1988, normally sedate foster parents across Canada threatened to strike if their demand for more money was not met. The child welfare agencies across the country, despite regional differences in practice and policy, supported them without reservation. The foster parents' primary complaint was that they were being treated ungratefully as a cheap dumping ground for society's problem children, without proper professional support. The rate paid by the provinces to foster parents (rates differ among provinces) runs around $15 per day per child, plus expenses. The younger the child, the less the parents get. Foster parents argued that they could make more money than that by providing daycare services to busy families, without the headaches of attempting to parent the children, without having to work around the clock caring for disturbed adolescents. Collectively, foster parents had reached an unprecedented level of frustration. But the crisis in foster care had been looming on the horizon for decades.

As early as 1963, disenchanted child advocates from Ottawa and Vancouver were signalling the imminent collapse of foster care. Social worker and researcher Jack Bevan suggested that competing agencies and institutions and changing socio-economic conditions were responsible for the declining number of foster homes. He cited foster parent frustrations with their limited therapeutic role, the deteriorating relationship between foster parents and social workers, and the consequent problems this posed for the children in their care.[2] Just over a decade later, Barbara Rosenblum, researching the plight of adolescents in foster homes, noted that the severe shortage of foster homes that was resulting in indiscriminate placement was detrimental to the welfare of wards of the state.[3] Throughout the next decade, as the number of foster homes continued to decline, a few solitary voices were heard warning the public and the child welfare professionals that child care resources were dwindling at a far quicker rate than they could be replaced. Still nobody appeared to listen, and frustrations continued to fester just beneath the surface. Children, then as now, suffered in obscurity.

In the United States, broad-scale investigations into out-of-home care initiated during the 1960s and '70s caused widespread public alarm. Congressional hearings were called, but, while highly motivated and well intended, they did little to change the life of children in care. Outspoken critics found that "increasingly many graduates of the foster care system evidence such severe emotional and behavioral problems that some thoughtful observers believe that foster care is often more harmful than the original home environment."[4] Marion Edelman, then president of the Children's Defense League of America, called the conditions of foster care a "national disgrace." Canada was apparently not seriously affected by these challenges to foster care south of the border.

It is impossible today to ignore this escalating crisis. In the past, though foster parenting associations have voiced their discontent with existing conditions, they have never had the wholesale support of the children's aid societies for whom they were working. Today, foster parents and state agencies both agree that with the steadily declining number of foster homes, increased burdens are being put upon all child intake services. Existing foster homes are becoming overcrowded. The more costly group and residential homes are being used more extensively, taxing already strained budgets. As well, inadequate funding and inconsistent implementation of programs that emphasize maintaining the family unit as long as possible are having unintended consequences: adolescents who do eventually come into care tend to arrive later and in an even more disturbed emotional state than if they had been removed sooner. Foster parents are not prepared to handle these types of adolescents.

It was this compounding of economic and social issues that led to the showdown in 1988 between the Ontario foster parents and child welfare agencies on one side and the Ontario Ministry of Community and Social Services, upon whom they rely for the bulk of their funds, on the other. This confrontation provoked a more explicit and hostile statement of the issues on which they differed, but didn't really bring out anything new. In 1987, Saskatchewan's social service ministry prepared a review of child welfare in that province, which anticipated the problems cited by the Ontario agencies. British Columbia, Alberta, and Manitoba were also waging the battle on their own terms. Newfoundland, in the wake of the Mount Cashel revelations, would follow. What was new in Ontario was the adversarial, public style of the debate, the outcome of which would determine the agenda of other provinces.

The Ontario Children's Aid Society (CAS) cited a 48 percent decrease in foster homes between 1980 and 1987, a statistic representative of the changes across Canada. In real numbers, that meant that in 1980 there were 19,632 beds available for displaced children; in 1987, there were less than 10,000. The CAS expected this trend to continue.[5] If foster parents already within the system became frustrated and left, and no recruits took their place, the foster parenting base would continue to crumble. With demand exceeding supply, the government could no longer guarantee adequate resources such as specialized treatment programs or homes.

On the surface the 1988 disagreement was a fight between government and its agencies (or between budgetary restraint and quality of service). It was also, on another level, a fight between the two allies, a fight by foster parents (the least institutionalized and professionalized of the rungs on the child care ladder) to solve the ongoing frustrations they experienced in their relationship with social service agencies. Foster parents were embittered by the condescending treatment they received from professional child advocates. They felt that they were not getting the respect they deserved and that their responsibilities were limited in capricious ways. Proper pay, though only a first step, would go a long way to assuage their concerns. At the very least, they argued, they should receive enough of an increase to cover all their expenses. Better pay, better training, and improved support systems — in short, status and recognition — would attract more qualified professionals into the fostering role. If these most reasonable improvements could not be made, fostering as a viable out-of-home placement was finished.

Thus, in 1988, child protection agencies and foster parent associations across the country presented a united front despite their internecine complaints. They lobbied and called press conferences to alert the public and force the government to respond to the crisis. In a March 1988 press conference in Toronto, the executive director of the Ontario Children's Aid Society, George Caldwell, openly challenged the niggardly federal and provincial commitments. The Ontario Children's Aid Society and the Ontario Foster Parenting Association in a joint statement condemned the provincial government for jeopardizing children's programs. Shortly thereafter, the minister of community and social services, John Sweeney, increased the daily stipend from approximately $15 to $17. The foster parents had asked for at least $26 by 1990.

Around this time the Ontario CAS issued a report that was intended to "provide the child and welfare field and the Ministry of Community and Social Services with an information base of immediate practical value for short-range planning and decision making."[6] Such was the stated aim, though the information contained in the study tended to serve the myopic interests of the Ontario Children's Aid Society. The report commented upon issues that had been under discussion for more than a decade: the frustrations of foster parents, the shortage of homes, the payment issue, and the consequences of these unsolved issues for children in care. It said very little that was new and nothing that could be taken as sincerely representative of the profound discontent that the children in the care of the Society were feeling. Indeed, in many instances it stated, or implied, that the children were "doing just fine."

What that report failed to convey to the government and to the public was that fostering doesn't work for the majority of the wards who depend upon it. It doesn't work because the assumptions and infrastructures designed to process these children through their school years and through puberty are sterile, middle-class, bureaucratic, and severely limited. It doesn't work because the system designed to care for these children is more intent on controlling than on nurturing them. It doesn't work because it forces a dependence upon the system that at age 16 or 18 it abruptly terminates, leaving the young people alone, unprepared, and confused. It doesn't work because the system is unwieldy and underregulated and its representatives frequently undereducated. It doesn't work because nobody has listened to the children. Perhaps most important, it doesn't work because those with whom the children spend the bulk of their time — the frustrated foster parents — are the least able to do anything for them. Foster care, its attendant residential programs, and the complex of organizational relationships that determine their success or failure, simply doesn't work according to its present design, and no amount of money is going to change that fact.

The system as it is currently designed treats children for all intents and purposes as robots, devoid of emotion, and it fails entirely to take their developmental needs into account, instead passing them off to those least trained to deal with them. The crisis, then, goes to the roots of the philosophy of what children are, how they grow to fit into society, and the meaning of protection, nurturance, maturation. To remove children from their parental homes, as the child protection agencies are increasingly able to do with little scrutiny, and place them in this ill-defined and frequently damaging child welfare system is itself abusive in a covert, and possibly more harmful, way. The child welfare system persistently and systematically discourages any feelings of worth, self-esteem, or confidence a child may have had upon entering the system. It virtually halts, or even reverses, the natural development of the person that must precede adulthood. Such a system is bound to turn out "products" that are the opposite of its stated intent.

For generations, children in care have been silent. Powerless, dependent upon the institutions and homes that demonstrated a callous disregard for their individuality and their special needs, children were deprived of all choice. Adults simply imposed their will upon these mute children. Those who were severely abused in their state-appointed homes were afraid to speak out for fear of retribution, and remained silent, uneducated, inarticulate, and isolated from other caring adults and even from their child peers in the "outside" world. It was that very isolation the system of care imposed upon them that ensured they would eventually emerge as "unfit" for society.

This appears to be changing. Now, after centuries of mute resignation, young people are beginning to make themselves heard. Encouraged by a small but growing number of professionals, and by a public sensitized to their plight through the highly publicized proceedings of several provincial inquiries, children in care are speaking with unanimity on what *they* think needs to be done. Aware of their rights and new-found freedoms under the Charter, and encouraged by their sense of self-empowerment, they want to make sure that we, and they, together figure out what this crisis entails and then solve it, because they are the ones who ultimately suffer the consequences of unsuccessful treatment.

The foster parents' 1988 threat of a mass exodus is a crude way of forcing the agencies who work with them (and the government that regulates and funds them) to undertake a comprehensive review of child protection and social service programs. Yet it may also be the only way to impress upon governments the need to challenge old assumptions and redesign service infrastructures based on bold new approaches. The crisis, however it is perceived, has made it necessary to re-examine the child protection system and to correct what many professionals now agree are long-standing and fundamental flaws.

Children's Aid, child welfare, "the Aid," as most kids in care call it — they all mean basically the same thing, but the perspective with which one views it depends upon one's place in its structure. Child care advocates speak of child welfare agencies such as the Ontario Children's Aid Society as the most advanced institution of its kind in the Western world for dealing with abandoned or neglected children. Many members of the general public think of it as just another subsidized charitable service to the less able members of society. The "less able" members served by it speak of it as an unwelcome instrument of the state upon which they and their children must, against their wishes, depend and which can intrude into their lives at any time.

Some of the children and adolescents who are the objects of intervention are abandoned by their parents, who are unwilling or unable to care for them. In some cases, the parents request state agencies to take the children off their hands. In still other cases, the children are forcibly removed from their home by the child protection agencies to "protect" them from their wayward guardians. Over 80 percent of these children are taken from the lower strata of society: from impoverished families, from the growing ranks of single mothers, from Native bands, and from the surging number of immigrant families. Due to a lack of preventive services designed to assist these marginal groups, and to very broad changes in society such as the break-up of the extended family, the number of households needing assistance with child rearing is increasing.

More than 200,000 troubled youths under 18 years of age are defined in the Canadian Child Welfare Act as emotionally disturbed, delinquent, neglected, or abandoned and in need of the assistance of the state. Approximately 60,000 of these youths become crown wards and depend solely upon the state for their well-being.[7] After terminating the parental rights, child protection authorities become responsible for providing all the things that a family would normally provide to the children: the physical amenities and the skills and the knowledge that will enable them to function in society. The state assumes the parental role and the attendant obligations.

The children are uncertain of the fate that awaits them in the netherland of what seems to them to be abandonment. Once removed, or consigned by their parents, and separated from their familiar environment and friends, they are surrounded by a new "extended family" consisting of a dizzying number of social workers, psychiatrists, therapists, doctors, shift after shift of group home and residential treatment staff — and, of course, their foster parents. As Chapter Three will document, foster parents, the people most closely associated with the child, are the least trained, the lowest paid, and the least professional within the field of child welfare.

Foster parents are the crucial element in the treatment plan for 60,000 of the nation's children. In this preferred setting the children are expected to find an ideal replacement for their parental home. It is left to the foster parents to mediate between the upset child and the overwhelmingly impersonal, bureaucratic world of the professional "helpers." While the foster parents are touted as the new parents and are therefore, in theory, the most important people in the child's reconstituted family life, in fact they act only as keepers, temporary guardians of children who will begin a life of transiency. Bonding — the emotional attachment of a child to a trusted adult, usually the mother — considered the most significant psychological element of a child's development, is actively discouraged in the majority of foster parent-child relationships. The children are only guests in their own home. The state, that vast web of agencies, departments, offices, and sub-departments, is the actual long-term parent. It is the *state*, through its professional representatives — psychiatrists, psychologists, and social workers — that makes the decisions that shape the child's life. Foster parents come to feel as though they are just carrying out orders, that they are mere workers on a long, disjointed assembly line with the children slowly moving past and onward. This confusing and contradictory role disenchants child and foster parents alike and very frequently leads to a breakdown in the placement — and another home. Disappointment, shattered expectations, and another move — these are the most common and the most debilitating features of life for a ward of the state.

What finally breaks a child's spirit is an accumulation of routine, seemingly harmless incidents. Often, a social worker with whom the foster child has developed an emotional bond moves beyond the range of duty — professional or geographical — to this particular child. For the social worker, the move is a career adjustment, a promotion perhaps, or a shuffling of their "caseload". For the child, it is one more abandonment, one more traumatic breach of trust, the cumulation of which etches deeper and deeper into his fragile mind the belief that he is essentially alone.

People working within the system are often the first to openly admit that it is not working. Considering the number of youths who had graduated from foster care, Dr. Elliot Barker, president of Canada's Society for the Prevention of Cruelty to Children, stated, "You show me a child that is moved to 10 different foster homes over a period of years and I'll show you a psychopath."

In a letter sent to Neil Webber, Alberta minister of social services and community health, in response to a call for information from professionals that would assist his department in making relevant changes in child welfare legislation, Dr. Gordon King, director of Children's and Adolescent Services in Alberta, wrote:

It has been apparent for many years and there was first-class hard data available that showed beyond a doubt that foster care and residential care were exceedingly expensive and ineffective ways of dealing with problem children, and there was not the slightest proof that these interventions were of any value generally, but even this was a matter of luck and not prediction.

I believe that we are now at the point where we can say with great confidence that intervention outside the home does not work, and this includes all modalities from the benign, cheap, head-start programs to the most expensive, destructive residential care for older children.[8]

In a similar vein, Dr. Paul Steinhauer, senior staff psychiatrist at Toronto's Hospital for Sick Children, wrote an influential paper pointing out the system's lack of long-term planning, its inappropriate use of resources, and the constant movement from place to place that left children and adolescents emotional wrecks.[9] Their inability to bond with other people because of this pattern of abandonments, he noted, resulted in profound psychological disturbances. The systemic flaws he was pointing to were dangerous enough when he was writing in 1979. They are worse today.

In the light of damning critiques from authorities within the child welfare system, we have no choice but to ask why we permit the state to intrude into a family's life. Under which circumstances can it succeed? And can we predict that success with any certainty? Can social workers perform their duty with any conviction when the system of which they are the gatekeepers is so offensive to many of their colleagues and certainly to the adolescents it was designed to help?

Traditionally, children over the age of 10, and "disturbed" or special-needs children, have been the most difficult to place. Today, these very children make up the bulk of the young people coming under the protection of the state. If there is a shortage of foster parents generally and trained foster parents specifically, who will care for these children? The mandate of social workers, and ultimately of the courts, is to act always "in the best interests of the child." But when is it in the best interests of children to remove them from a family and place them in a system that lacks the resources and the means to care for them? At what point does the state become accountable for its failure to meet the obligations of its assumed parental role? The answers to these crucial questions will determine the fate of coming generations of foster children.

2

CARING

My mom put me in the Children's Aid when I was seven or eight. She took me down there and I remember sitting with these two women and my mom was telling them all about her problems and how I was so difficult to handle. I was crying. She didn't once say anything about my problems. She just didn't want to handle me. She told me she had already put up with two of us and she didn't have to put up with another ingrate. She always used to call me an ingrate. I went to seven different families and two group homes before getting out of there.

In some ways maybe it was better getting away from my mom. But I don't know. You don't have anything except your mom when you're little. My brother and sister were way older, and they were never around when I was little. I don't even know them that much now. Every year I would be in a different school and every year I got quieter and quieter. I was never bad. I have to say that. I am not a bad person. I used to think I was and I know I've done bad things, but I'm not a bad person. I wasn't very outgoing or anything so I didn't have a lot of friends, but I wasn't bad.

I always felt out of place. Kids would ask me where I live and I would tell them and somehow it would get out that I lived with foster parents and that would do something. They'd say nasty things or just leave me off to the side. They sort of laughed or said things, and so I felt out of things, never really part of it.

I tried to commit suicide when I was 11, twice. First time I took a whole bunch of pills, all different kinds, and I went to bed and I left a note. I still got it. I told my mom I was sorry for being the way I was and I told Bev and Dennis [the foster parents] that it wasn't their fault. I told them how sad I was. And then I went to bed. The next morning I woke up and I kept looking around and feeling myself. I couldn't believe I was still alive. My note was still there. And I thought I can't even kill myself.

Then when I was 12 I tried to slit my wrists and they found me and sent me to the psychiatric ward and they brought my mom in and the social worker and a lot of people and I wouldn't talk to anyone except my mom and I begged her to take me home. So I spent a year going to psychiatrists and group therapy, where you sit with a lot of other kids and talk about your problems. That was pretty good really 'cause I got to talk with other kids who were just like me. I began to think that it wasn't really me who was so bad, it was the situation, you know my mom, and the homes. The only two who were nice to me, who really liked me, were Bev and Dennis, and I could never figure out why I tried to kill myself there. Bev told me later that she knew I'd done something 'cause the pills were gone. I still talk to them. But the others. . . . I don't know. I just never felt part of their families. After a while you just shut yourself off 'cause you know it isn't going to last anyway. . . .

I was living with my mom when I first became pregnant. I was 15. I was going out with Randy. My mom hated Randy. Whenever he came over she'd go out of her way to be nasty to both him and me. She'd belittle me in front of him, telling him what a slob I was and that I'd never become anything and then she'd turn on him and tell him that he was a no-good anyway and that he deserved what he got. Randy was really kind to me. He wanted me to get out of there. He could see what she was like. He said he would take care of me.

One day I came home after being with him. It was pretty late and my mom says where were you. Screams it out at the top of her voice and starts slapping me. And she has a friend there and she starts telling her that I'm a slut and all kinds of things. And I knew right then that I was gone. I couldn't fight her. I'm not like that. I just went to my room and started crying, laying on my bed and crying and crying. That evening I had told Randy that I was pregnant and he was so happy and I was happy then because he was. I got my clothes together and a few things. I didn't have any money and I called Randy and he came by and picked me up. I didn't leave a note for my mother or anything. Didn't tell her I was pregnant.

About two weeks go by and Randy and I found a place on our own and we began living together. Randy was so good. He was 19, working steady. He wanted to get us a house. I got part-time work for a little while.

Strange, though, after a little while I missed my mom. I wanted to let her know I was pregnant and so I phoned one day about halfway through and she was real happy to hear from me. She said how sorry she was and sometimes when she was drinking she lost control of herself and, you know, that kind of thing and then I told her I was pregnant. She thought I was too young to take on that kind of responsibility, but it was too late now and she wouldn't mind having a little grandson. She was clear about that. She wanted a boy and not a girl. For the last months just before I had Mark she was really good and so was Randy. She bought little things and told me things about the baby, feeding and changing and things like that. And Randy would come home with little gifts for me. I think that was the happiest period of my life.

Then I had Mark. He was a real fussy one. He was
crying all the time and waking up a lot. For the first two
months I hardly slept. My mom said he was a little colic,
the worst kind. That's how I was, she said. She didn't
come around too much. Randy tried to do things, but he
was a bit nervous. He wondered if I had done something
or if something was wrong with the baby. So a lot of the
time I was alone. I remember the first time I ever hit
Mark. He was three months old and I was tired and it
didn't seem that anything I did was right. I used to yell at
him a lot, but that's all, just yell or close the door and
just leave him there. And then one day I just belted him.
I mean really hit him and threw him off the bed.

Well he yelled harder after that and I couldn't believe
what I had done. He had the mark of my hand across his
face and I picked him up off the floor and he was
screaming and I told him how sorry I was and that it was
my nerves and I began crying too. Randy saw the mark
when he came home and I told him that he fell. We
weren't getting along great 'cause my nerves weren't
great from lack of sleep and worrying about the baby
and Randy was gone a lot of the time. I'd go to my mom
and she'd just say I told you you shouldn't have had a
baby. By the time Mark was a year old I probably had
beat him about twenty times. I can't tell you what that
feels like after. You can't believe it and you know you'll
never do it again and you do and then you feel awful and
then you do it again.

So I went to the Children's Aid and I asked to see
someone there and they gave me this counsellor, a social
worker, and they got me into a baby program. After a
while I told her what I had been doing. She was horrified. I mean horrified. She took the baby for a medical.
And she had me monitored real close. I said I didn't
want it, that I couldn't take care of him. She really tried
to help me, but finally I just said please, he's yours, can't

someone else take care of him who won't do this to him. I knew it was better for him as well as for me.

He'll be nine next month. I really love him and all that and I want to see him. I keep my name on the register [parent register for foster children seeking their real parents] in case he wants to find me one day. I wish I wasn't the way I was. Now I've got nobody. Nobody.[1]

Permanency planning in foster care, which is meant to overcome the initial trauma of separation from the parent, is based primarily on the pioneering work of John Bowlby and his successors. Bowlby was influenced by animal psychologist H.F. Harlow. While other theories and perspectives hold sway in the treatment of adolescents, the concept of bonding and separation is the hallmark of intervention and the basis for legislative direction and policy regarding the treatment of children in care.

In a series of experiments during the late 1940s and '50s, Harlow placed infant monkeys in environments where they depended for their sustenance on two artificial surrogate mothers, each of whom was incomplete in a different way. The setting was a cage. One surrogate could provide nourishment but was cold, made of wire-mesh, and electrically controlled. (Thus, in the most rudimentary sense, food and shelter, basic animal needs, were supplied.) The second surrogate was a shapeless, soft terry-cloth bundle that provided nothing in the way of food; it was there for the infant monkey to snuggle against.

Harlow's studies demonstrated that infant monkeys raised in the presence of these artificial surrogates invariably preferred the "warm", soft cloth mothers, even though they received no nourishment from these but got all of their life-sustaining food from the wire-mesh mother. When frightened or tired, they clung to the terry-cloth version, seeking from it an expression of the warmth they felt and needed in "her" body.

Harlow and his associates established further experimental situations in which all the ingredients presumed essential for physiological development were supplied. They designed controlled, comfortable environments with food, water, warmth — everything needed to sustain life — but excluding the presence of another animal or human. What was missing in all cases was a parental figure, even a surrogate. The creatures that emerged from these environments were, from a behavioural viewpoint, almost unidentifiable as being "of their own kind."

The subjects engaged continuously in odd, unpredictable, and autistic behaviours. They did not seem attentive or in some cases alive. The more severe the lack of contact with creatures of their own species, the more severely disturbed the behaviour. After less than three months of deprivation, behaviour could be reversed. But animals isolated for a period as short as six months were permanently damaged.[2]

Relating this series of experiments to human psychosocial development, Harlow theorized that the features most closely associated in the human animal with its humanness — the capacity to enjoy and become a member of a social unit, to have and display deeply felt emotions, to be able to play and to learn — were absent. The experiments suggested that just as there are certain basic necessities for the maintenance of life, so there are certain requirements that are not merely desirable but are essential for the development of psychological and intellectual well-being. Without them, the personality — the soul — if not the person, dies. Harlow concluded from his studies that socialization is the key factor in determining the degree of security and the ability to engage in relationships that will develop.

Harlow's pioneering studies shocked the scientific community. Social science disciplines began to explore the relationship between infant bonding and later stages of development, and the work of John Bowlby emerged as seminal. He did for early child deprivation theorists what Freud had done for psychology in general.

Bowlby and his associates began studying babies who had

been torn from their parents by war or other enforced separations.[3] Most of these children were in their second or third year
of life and were cared for in hospitals or residential nurseries in
which they had no mother substitute. During his work Bowlby
was "deeply impressed by the intensity of the distress and
misery he witnessed whilst the children were away from home
and the extent and duration of the disturbance that was present
after they had returned there."[4]

In his voluminous papers he showed that "loss of the
mother figure during infancy is capable of generating depres-
sive, hysterical, or psychopathic traits in adults." Like Harlow,
he concluded that if bonding does not take place during the
earliest period of infancy, or if it is cut off prematurely, sometimes exaggerated nurturance during the childhood years can
partially compensate for it. However, Bowlby cautioned that
an early break in the continuity of the emotional relationship
seriously disturbs the potential for normal development.
Bowlby's ongoing studies influence the present generation of
social workers and psychologists working in the field of child
development.

Dr. Freda Martin, a psychologist who studied with Bowlby
and now heads a Toronto clinic treating disturbed adolescents,
suggests that by the time an abused or "unbonded" child is
eight years of age, intervention is probably too late. She points
out that

> it costs about $2,000 per year to intervene effectively
> when an infant is unstable. It costs $9,000 per year to
> help a 10-year-old cope at school. It costs about $50,000
> per year to keep a disturbed adolescent in a treatment
> centre. The price of dealing with a rapist or self-abusive
> woman is incalculable.[5]

The degree of abuse and neglect that youth in care have
suffered varies greatly. But it is generally held that the more
severe the abuse, the more severe the psychological consequences. Youth in care show signs of depression, confusion
about sexual roles or identity, low self-esteem, an unwilling-

ness or inability to form relationships with peers and adults, and aggression. These personal inadequacies combined with the confusions generated by their abandonment compound their inappropriate responses both to those who are trying to help them and to their peers. It follows that they, much more than children in biological families, need stability and nurturance.

In the years following Bowlby's work, leading child advocates argued for permanency planning in foster care as the single most critical element in successful intervention. If the state could not offer a permanent placement ensuring the possibility of bonding with surrogate parents, then the state should not be allowed to intervene.[6] This theory is purportedly the guiding principle behind court decisions on whether to remove a child from the parental home. Social service agencies have to prove that the state's home is measurably better than the child's home. If they could not guarantee permanence, they could not make a convincing case that the state's substitute home was better than the child's original home. This principle was meant to limit the authority of the state to intervene in and disrupt the family, while also assuring those children who were abused or neglected and in need of permanent, stable out-of-home placement that they would get them. Unfortunately, this widely acknowledged principle has not had a noticeable effect on Canadian attempts to provide stable alternative homes. Transiency remains the predominant characteristic of children and adolescents dependent upon the state.

This has a severely disturbing effect upon the adolescent's sense of identity and self-esteem. Abandoned or abused by their own families, separated repeatedly from homes throughout their sojourn with the social agency, they feel they don't belong anywhere, to anyone. Of course, no child wants to spend his or her entire life known as so-and-so's son or daughter. But the early identification with parents and siblings gives children practice in forming an identity. Later, of course, they will build upon and surpass that first base when forming their more mature concept of themselves as some*one*. In contrast, a child who was unable to form a comfortable identity as belonging to so-and-so lacks the ability to creatively shape a satisfying sense of self as a unique and worthwhile individual.

Even if one doubted some specifics of Bowlby's theory of bonding (which most child advocates do not), it is hard to discount the effects of discontinuity that most of these young people face. Establishing identity through ties to kin and tribe is a universal human trait, observable in all historical and cultural milieus. Most sacred and classical texts that come down to us from antiquity (the Bible and Homer's *Odyssey* being two examples) present their heroes with extensive genealogies; the naming of the forefathers sometimes goes on for pages. Without such histories, the characters lacked legitimacy. Even today, anthropologists find that prestige and status within communities in non-industrialized societies are conditional upon family identity and are the most important feature of those people's lives. The more cohesive the clan, the more rich and varied the cultural symbols that they share. Individuals lacking this rich, historical sense of identity have a status more as permanent guest, or only indentured servant, than as fellow tribespeople.

Foster children belong neither to their natural family nor to the state-appointed surrogate. Lacking a full sense of identity, they often come across as hollow nonentities compared with their more culturally integrated schoolmates. When such children reach an age at which they become conscious of their identity (or lack of one), they struggle to fill the void with images or models scrounged from the dust heaps of society's imaginings: the simplified but glamorous images of good guy/ bad guy, insider/outsider, macho killer and villain. They become the abuser, or the abused. This is precisely what happens when a pimp exploits a vulnerable girl's need for love, relationship, identity. And when their adopted image fails to yield fulfilment, such youths lash out in anger and rage at those near them — peers, or authority figures — or at themselves. Lacking an identity that makes them one of a larger group, they have no inhibition against acting against those with whom they have no essential connection, no empathy, no commonality.

In her analysis of psychopathic personalities, child psychiatrist Selma Fraiberg points out that many mental diseases

> are produced in the early years by the absence of human ties or the destruction of human ties. In the absence of human ties those mental qualities that we call human will fail to develop or will be grafted upon a personality that cannot nourish them, *so that at best they will be imitations of virtues, personality façades* [italics mine].[7]

This theory echoes the findings of Dr. John Bowlby and Anna Freud, who suggested that if a child fails to find an adequate mother within a critical period of time, his energy may become overinvested in his own inner world of fantasy, which then assumes more importance for him than reality. "This," writes Bowlby, "will lead to a progressive withdrawal and an increasing turning for gratification to fantasy rather than to real experiences or other people."[8]

On average, foster children experience four placements before they become adults, though some have moved through as many as 18 different homes. These separations undoubtedly exacerbate the turmoil caused by the original separation from biological parents and compound its detrimental effects if the original frustrations were dealt with inappropriately. Foster children need to feel more than anything else that they are bonded to the human beings around them, that they are an integral part of a familial grouping, that they would be missed if they were not there.

Since its inception, foster parenting has been based on the idea that the family is the natural place for orderly and healthy growth to occur. Despite the rhetoric of nurturance and establishing long-term relationships in which bonding can reoccur between the child and a trusted adult, foster parents are warned not to become too attached to the child since it is possible that the child will be returned to his natural family, or that the placement for some other reason will be only temporary. In theory, foster parents are expected to provide the child with "sufficient and suitable food, bed . . .; opportunity to attend school and attend religious services; receive medical care . . . and all the emotional benefits of a true new member of the family." But contractual arrangements contradict that optimistic role. They invariably emphasize that

> the child in question is placed on a temporary board and care basis only and not placed with the family for adoption; [and] that the welfare commissioner or agency reserve the right to remove the child at any time from the foster home and that upon such removal the initial agreement is canceled immediately.[9]

Anna Dobbs, a former foster parent in Vancouver, speaks for many foster parents in her expressed confusion over her pseudo-parental role.

> I get a kid and I want to try my best to make them part of the family — I've got two of my own — but I know that it's only temporary so I don't want the kid's hope built up, so I tell him just what he can and can't do and that for the time he is with us he is just one of us. And I mean it. Or I want to. But I can't make the decisions for him that I would make for my own child. I can't really treat him like my own. Maybe I can get close, but even here I'm leery. I don't want to get too close because he is going to go, right? And so this tension is built into the relationship. He gets pissed off 'cause I'm one more in the string of homes he's been through, in all of which, no doubt, he was told he was just one of the family. I'm just like his mother, he says, or I'm just like his social worker. He says that I don't really care. And I get frustrated because I really do care. But it ends up that I'm just like everyone else he's encountered along the way. It's hard. I tried to do the best I could within the limits.

Thus foster parents are compelled to play two contradictory roles. On the one hand, they are to replace the family as the psychological parents. And in this sense they represent the best intention of foster care. On the other hand, they are told they are caretakers only. The resulting confusions combined with the transience of the child's passage through the foster/institutional system undermines the possibility of bonding.

The same self-defeating impermanence saps the professional relationships of their effectiveness. Dr. Paul Steinhauer, of Toronto's Hospital for Sick Children, suggests that this transiency may be unavoidable. In his article, *"How to Succeed in the Business of Creating Psychopaths Without Even Trying,"* he warned social workers of the need to distance themselves from their charges, rather than risk facing burnout. He stated:

> One of the professional hazards he [social service provider] faces is that of being contaminated by feelings of despair, helplessness, and hopelessness emanating from his patients. Children's Aid workers, like physicians, can easily become trapped in the mire of their client's chronic depression, losing their objectivity and initiative. . . . It is essential to remain aware at all times of one's separateness from the child and family, avoiding the contagion of their depression.[10]

The desire to remain separate, while understandable, and perhaps necessary in certain circumstances for the health of the social worker, is antithetical to the need of the child and the theory of bonding. It implicitly suggests that the child protection services as we now deploy them can be only caretaking institutions, warehouses for unwanted children, and not environments for nurturing children to maturity. To try to do so would result in burnout and loss of objectivity. Steinhauer goes on to state that healing is a grandiose scheme, a sign of naivete.

Although Steinhauer elsewhere in his writings has acknowledged that the primary need of a child in care is to know that he belongs and that he is important to someone, directing social workers to maintain their "separateness from the child and family" would give the child a clear message that he is separate, a solitary atom in the universe.

Our deepening insight into childhood development and its stages has shown the significance for later life of another pair of personality traits in addition to those of permanence and bonding, namely, dependence and independence. A child who enters the state system almost invariably veers far towards the unhealthier of the two.

To become dependent is to become vulnerable. Dependence presumes a relationship between powerful and powerless persons. It is a precarious state encountered by all human beings during infancy. What Bowlby's and Harlow's studies point to, by implication at least, is that being a recipient of care during the early stages of life is a prerequisite for later strength and independence, and conversely, that dependence betrayed by abuse makes it *im*possible later for a person to achieve a proper balance between dependence and independence.

Willard Gaylin, an American psychologist, comments on this aspect of development.

> This period of early infancy is the crucible and forge in which the potential of an animal is molded and shaped into the model of its kind — or damaged or destroyed. . . . During this state the child is incapable of performing activities because he simply does not have the equipment to do so. In addition, many of the developed parts of the neonate are present, but only in a state of extreme and delicate vulnerability, dependent on the proper environment in order to mature and develop; with an inappropriate environment they can atrophy and be destroyed.[11]

The archetypal model of dependence, of the relationship between the powerful and the powerless, is the mother-child relationship. The adult, in the eyes of the infant, is all-powerful, and if all goes well she will care for her child, putting all her formidable capacities at his disposal. The child learns gradually, through small disappointments and playground betrayals, the dangers of too open a vulnerability, but the defences he builds are proportionate to and counterbalanced by other, happier experiences of generosity and "unearned" care. The child is thus prepared to enter — albeit with proper caution — adult dependencies: dependence upon lover or spouse, employer or partner, teacher, expert, legal official, and so on. Whatever discomfort or danger arises from submitting to these authorities in some of life's events is balanced by the person's own properly developed sense of selfhood, their own training and talents, their own superiority in other of their adult relationships.

The uniquely extended period of dependence that characterizes human infants suggests that we, more than any other animal, are in need of active, profound, and long-standing caring, both physical and emotional, from the adults around us. In the optimal caring encounter, the infant's first contact will be with the mother: the milk of her breast, the warmth and smell of her body, the immediate satisfying of hunger as a result of her constant ministrations. If that contact is solid and consistent, the child begins to coo his delight. He will form what Joseph Chilton Pearce, following Piaget, has called the matrix — a sort of exterior emotional womb — on which all further relationships between himself and the outside world will be based.

This initial dependence, as rewarded by the love of the mother, is the essential basis from which, in a natural progression, the child moves out to explore his environment, feeling safe and secure. Gradually the child begins ordering the features of the world around him. Attention shifts from his biological needs to the more abstract areas of the relationship with the adults around him. While the mother remains the focus for those first months, gradually the father begins to assume a recognized nurturing role. Again, the safety and the security necessary for those first hesitant explorations are simply "assumed" by the infant. He can be dependent safely. During this period the psychological imprints that will guide his development are established. The caring attitudes of the parents remain the foundation upon which the child's personality is formed.

For much of his first seven years the child will be play learning: that is, his link with the world will be imitative and imaginative. Much of this development will take place in the family setting, upon which he models his relationships with those outside, his peers and others in the community. He will learn the language, the shared system of meanings that will enable him to communicate effectively with a wide range of people. By age seven, according to Piaget, the child begins to conceptualize, a new feature of mental life that will catapult him into new relationships with the outside world. He will form mental "pictures" of new, more abstract objects and situations, gradually developing more complex metaphors or maps of reality that are the concepts of mature adult thinking. Parents in positive and close relationships, recognizing the shifting, stage-by-stage development of the infant to child to adolescent, provide a secure framework from which the young person will eventually emerge.

Throughout this period, sibling and other peer relationships affect the child's world. He learns to share and to feel protective and protected. He learns that he is responsible for his actions. He will come to learn that his family has roots in history, that his forefathers had some bearing on his present circumstances. He understands that his family extends beyond his home. He will hear tales of the family's exploits, its heroes, its tragedies. He will learn of marriage outside the family and deaths within it. By the time he reaches adolescence, with the support of his family he will have been socialized into the large community via its various programs — schools, recreational activities, neighbourhoods — and will have learned to interact with this larger community of which he is a part.

At some point during the turbulent adolescent years he will wean himself from the control of his parents and find his own internal source of independence. He will consider the alternatives open to him in the future, consider what effect particular choices will have upon him and upon those around him. He will become someone capable of caring not only about himself and his family but also about the world in which he has roots and for the future of the world to which he belongs. In time he will marry, produce children, and, following the nurturant model that his parents and family had provided, he too will begin the process of raising the next generation. If along the way unavoidable troubles overwhelm him, he can rely upon the resources and collective knowledge of his family, friends, and community to help him through.

An ideal history, granted. But it is really only a more collo-quial revision of Abraham Maslow's well-known theory of psychological development. Maslow suggested that only when all the lower or basic needs are met — food, shelter, and sleep — can one go on to fulfil the higher developmental needs of inner growth, those that are met by partaking in civic responsi-bility, aesthetic appreciation, philosophical discourse, in short, in one's culture and religion.

Maslow's evidence for this more advanced developmental model was gathered during many years of studying creative, expansive, productive individuals who frequently experienced what Maslow termed "peak" moments, a kind of exuberant sense of well-being that for some of them bordered on the mystical, and for all of them centred on a highly creative mode of thought and feeling. Without exception, each of these adults described loving childhoods; not necessarily stable, but always nurturant. Their basic needs during their dependent state were satisfied to an exceptional degree.

The development of the abused child moves in precisely the opposite direction. When early relationships, most impor-tantly the mother-child relationship, go askew, when the mother abuses her power and takes advantage of the child's vulnerability, the maturation process is stymied and the child fails to receive proper models upon which he can later base his own relationships of either controlled power or appropriate submission. If the child is physically harmed, or his emotional needs are ignored in his early years, he will learn that the state of dependency is always dangerous. The child will seek to avoid such a state by running away from home, isolating himself, or by taking on in self-defence the superficial traits of maturity before being ready to exercise them in socially acceptable ways. In the most severe cases, he will become autistic. The young adult will be fearful of entering close personal relationships because intimacy requires openness and self-revelation, and that makes one vulnerable. He may also lack the ability to form a relationship of any kind. Instead, he may seek to be authoritarian and invulnerable, trying to maintain an aura of impervious strength by engaging in barroom brawls or beating his girlfriend.

Unfortunately, a vicious circle is set when the child reaches adulthood, when the personal psychological inadequacies develop a more social aspect. For if the child who has avoided dependence has not submitted to the routines of school or apprenticeship, and thus to the subtle relationships of master-learner that are a necessary preparation for life, the person will almost inevitably end up still dependent upon others — on his own parents again for support, on the state for welfare and unemployment cheques, on the good graces of police or parole officers. These adult dependencies are even more frustrating, more embarrassing, and more insulting, finally, to his self-esteem than the original childhood dependencies. And so the adult lashes out in fury at the authority figures, and, unable to accept any form of authority, merely prolongs and ensures a stultifying, destructive dependency. Child advocates throughout the Western world accept as an axiom the direct relationships between abuse in childhood and an inability to achieve a healthy mix of dependence and independence in adulthood, which requires trust on the one hand and confidence on the other.

By coupling Piaget's preprogrammed or genetically imprinted stage-development model of conceptual learning with Maslow's hierarchical model of emotional development, we get a fuller picture of the kind of caring that is the *sine qua non* of healthy personal development. Individuation, or psychological integration, requires a stable, nurturant base. Needless to say, children in care stand little chance of receiving these prerequisites or of developing according to these ideal models.

They perceive themselves to be outsiders among their schoolmates and are dependent upon, though only loosely bonded to, a variety of social-service providers. They fear their superiors because of their vulnerability, yet they lack the power or encouragement to make their own decisions. The realities of adult life will either crush them in limp submission or force them into angry eruption.

Adolescents who have gone through the foster system speak of feeling that they belong to no one. One youth I interviewed said bleakly, "It isn't good if you ain't got no one. And I got no one." Another, 15 and living on the street, shouted, "I've been living on the street since I was a baby." When pressed for an elaboration, he scowled, "The Aid, jerk, I been in the Aid since I was just a kid, and that ain't no different to this here" — pointing to the street. This quality of rootlessness, of belonging neither to a family nor to history, is so deeply imbedded in the psyches of many foster children that I came to view them as suffering from a common disease, perhaps the most acute form of a peculiarly modern affliction, an existential dread that runs through modern literature as the leitmotif of the twentieth century. In philosophy and popular culture this existential dread has been analyzed as a feeling of abandonment by God, the metaphysical equivalent of having been abandoned by one's parents. But for the unlettered children in care, no brave analysis or intellectual comforts exist to alleviate the very real visceral fear and emotional confusion that follow abandonment. Like the monkeys in Harlow's experiments, they act as though they are not really one of our own kind. There are no family photograph albums, no graduation diplomas, no milestones to mark the transitions, no figures who remain constant through their lives. They live in an ahistorical world, in which rejection and abandonment are all they can expect.

Our responsibility as care givers, or as concerned citizens, to this vulnerable population is to minimize their fear, to maximize the potential for bonding in order to make them whole again. Anything less is a betrayal.

3

THE SYSTEM

I asked you for help
and you told me you would
if I told you the things
my dad did to me.
It was really hard for me
to say all those things
but you told me to trust you.
Then you made me repeat them
to fourteen different strangers.

I asked you for privacy
and you sent two policemen
to my school in front of everyone
to "go downtown" for a talk
in their black and white car
like I was the one being busted.

I asked you to believe me
and you said that you did.
Then you connected me to a lie detector
and took me to court where lawyers
put me on trial like I was a liar.
I can't help it if I can't remember times and dates
or explain why I couldn't tell my mom.
Your questions got me confused —
my confusion got you suspicious.

I asked you for help
and you gave me a doctor
with cold metal gadgets and cold hands.
Who spread my legs and stared just like my father.
Who said it wouldn't hurt, just like my father.
Who said not to cry, just like my father.
He said I looked fine —
Good news for me, you said
bad news for my "case".

I asked you for confidentiality
and you let the newspapers get my story.
What does it matter that they left my name out
when they put in my father's
and our home address?
Even my best friend's mother
won't let her talk to me anymore.

I asked for protection
and you gave me a social worker
who patted me and called me "Honey"
mostly because she could never remember my name.
She sent me to live with strangers
in another place with a different school.
I lost my part in the school play and the science fair
while my father and others all got to stay home.

Do you know what it's like to live
where there's a lock on the refrigerator,
where you have to ask permission to use the shampoo
and where you can't use the phone to call your friends?
You get used to hearing, "Hi, I'm your new social
worker,
This is your new foster sister, dorm mother, group
home."
You tiptoe around like a perpetual guest
and don't even get to see your own puppy grow up.

Do you know what it's like
to have more social workers than friends?

Do you know what it feels like
to be the one that everyone blames for all the trouble?
Even when they were speaking to me
all they talked about was lawyers, shrinks, fees
and whether they'll lose the mortgage.
Do you know what it's like
when your sisters hate you
and your brother calls you a liar?
It's my word against my own father's.
I'm twelve years old
and he's the manager of a bank.
You say you believe me —
who cares if nobody else does?

I asked you for help
and you forced my mom to choose between us.
She chose him of course.
She was scared and had a lot to lose.
I had a lot to lose too.
The difference was you never told me how much.

I asked you to put an end to the abuse.
You put an end to my whole family.
You took away my nights of hell
and gave me days of hell instead.
You've exchanged my private nightmare for a very public
nightmare.

*Former foster child (poem from the National Youth in
Care Network Archives)*

Who are the kids who trundle like wind-blown tumble-
weeds through our child welfare system? What kinds of

homes do they come from? What sets them apart from people raised in "normal", healthy families? These are some of the questions that will be addressed in this chapter, which will look in more detail at the three major components of the system: the kids, the foster parents, and the child care workers.

In North America, more than half a million children are in foster care. Canada has more than 60,000 crown wards in foster care, with approximately 12,000 a year entering and leaving the system.[1] For long-term wards — that is, for children whose parents' rights have been terminated — adoption is the placement of choice. However, given the public's unwillingness to adopt older children, foster care is usually where they end up. A series of studies in the late 1970s established that children who remain in care beyond "one to one-and-one-half years have a sharply reduced chance of ever being restored to their parents."[2]

Statistics from across Canada illustrate that approximately one-third of children in care are there because their parents are unable to care for them, usually as a result of mental or physical illness or family problems, this last often tied to alcoholism. Another third are admitted because their parents are unwilling to care for them — that is, in many cases parents, or more often single mothers, voluntarily approach an agency and ask to be relieved of the stress of caring for their child. The remaining third are removed from their homes voluntarily, or by the courts as a consequence of abuse, neglect, or abandonment. Clearly, then, most children are not in care because they are bad or delinquent, though they may be troubled by the time they enter the system. In the vast majority of cases they had no choice. The decision was made for them either by their parents or by the authorities.[3]

An increasing number of children are entering the system on the wave of current events. Due to mounting public awareness of sexual and physical abuse, public education programs, and mandatory reporting laws, more and more investigations into abuse are launched. Every Canadian province reports increases of 500 to 1,000 percent over the last decade in the number of abuse allegations; most of these have to do with sexual abuse. Given the great repulsion our society feels for sexual abuse, we have allowed social workers unprecedented latitude to apprehend children whom they have reason to believe are or will be sexually abused. Whereas current provincial legislation (such as the Ontario Child and Family Service Act and similar acts in most provinces) encourages the reunification of the family as the primary goal of intervention, in practice, the reality during sexual abuse investigations is to remove the child and assume parental guilt first, which quickly results in adversarial relationships within the family. Since we now know that a significant number of children are indeed sexually abused, this course of action is preferred to leaving the young girl or boy in a potentially dangerous situation.

However, the child welfare system lacks the resources and expertise to deal with the increasing number of sexually abused children coming into care. It is the children, as always, who suffer from inadequate treatment programs and haphazard methods of planning once they are removed from their natural homes.

But whether it is the decision of the parents or of the court to remove them from their natural homes and place them in state-sponsored homes, these youths, who are often unable to anticipate the changes in their environment or comprehend the sudden uprooting, become frightened, demanding, depressed, or rebellious. They begin to lash out at foster parents, who are not expecting this response to their sincere attempts to help. Frequently the placement breaks down. The children's anger is interpreted within the system as a behavioural defect or a management problem. The gloomy information is written into their charts; it becomes a label that will follow them through the system. By the time a child reaches his third placement, all behaviour, warranted or not, will be seen in the context of the label affixed to his chart. The psychiatrist or psychologist who diagnoses problems and suggests treatment relies upon this hearsay evidence and the observations of untrained foster parents, upon social workers who spend, on average, a paltry one

hour per month with the child, and upon the accumulating list
of judgments that accompanies the child. The label serves to
interpret the behaviour the youth exhibits, and comes to represent the child to all those who come in contact with him. The
system is constructed in such a way that children with a wide
range of problems must be treated by a narrow range of services; it is inevitable that service providers conveniently catego-
rize their clientele into neat little packages.

In the 1988 study mentioned earlier, *The Future of Foster
Care*, sponsored by the Ontario Children's Aid Society, an
attempt was made to put into perspective the services now
available for children and what will be needed over the coming
years. Fourteen Societies from across Ontario, incorporating
rural and urban areas, participated, including Peterborough,
Timmins, Toronto, Brockville, Hamilton, and North Bay. The
bulk of the report deals with the responses to questionnaires
sent out to foster parents, foster children, and social workers.
Additional background information was compiled through
Statistics Canada and related child welfare data bases. Various
other studies initiated by governments in the last few years
provide a background to the report and offer a comparative
base over the past decade.

According to the results, today's "average" foster child is
likely to be a 12-year-old male, in grade seven. He was admitted
to care at about nine or ten years of age and has had fewer than
three placements. The number of males is generally slightly
higher than the number of females in care at any given time.
The family breakdown that precipitated his admission into
care will continue, leaving him in care until he reaches 18 years
of age. He exhibits behaviour-management problems and
maintains a low education-achievement level. Most youths
who enter the system are said to require long-term care.

Children can be removed from their homes for a wide variety of reasons, including poor housekeeping by the parents,
alcoholism or heavy drinking by the parents, being born out of
wedlock, and of course many reasons related to outright abuse.
Single mothers, a large majority of whom require social assist-

ance, are becoming reluctant to approach child welfare authorities, despite their needs, because they are afraid that the authorities will remove their children. Monica Rosenberg recently sued the British Columbia government over its flat-rate maintenance fee, which prevented her from receiving child support from her ex-husband. She called it a trap for single mothers who were handicapped by divorce and saddled with kids whom they want to care for while also trying to better themselves, but who are unable to receive help from anyone.

> I'm not skilled. I can work for $4 per hour and believe me, I've done it all, but how am I going to pay for day care, or babysitters? How am I going to get around? I want to retrain. Where am I going to get the money? Cars and public transport cost money. How am I going to get my kids from one place to the other, while I go off and work for $4 an hour? It's just a vicious cycle. I'm forced to go on welfare and I'm forced to stay there. You can get mad and refuse to accept their money on principle, but what then? Where does that get you? If you don't take the money you end up giving your kids away to the government anyway; how else are they going to get fed and clothed? And when you get a chance, they penalize you for taking money from your ex or your family that allows you to get out of the trap. It's so degrading.[4]

Welfare policies seem unable to find a way to break the cycle by providing enough assistance so that either out-of-home work is not necessary or the children receive proper care while the mother is at work.

Because clear guidelines do not exist, the individual biases of judges and social workers play a prominent role in their decisions to remove children from their natural homes. A recent case in Toronto illustrates that bad decisions can be made because of snap judgments. A handicapped couple who had been together for 12 years were assessed as incompetent by a Society worker after three visits. The worker indicated that the husband had a record of aggression and brutality, that the house was filthy and the children unmanageable. The couple, she indicated, were resistant to change. The couple countered that although the husband had been abusive many years earlier, he had not displayed such behaviour since then, and that the worker made the mother nervous: she suspected that she was being judged, consequently suffered stress during the period when the social worker visited and accordingly fell down in her level of housecleaning and control of the children. The children became unmanageable, the couple argued, only when the social worker threatened to remove them from the house. They begged their parents not to let the social worker take them away. The husband was also said to be hysterical, an assessment made because he said in desperation, as the worker was leaving with his two children, "If you take them I'll kill myself." "What would you do," he said later, "if somebody ran off with your two kids you tried eight years producing? That was our life being taken away." The couple is currently fighting to regain custody.[5]

Once removed from his natural home, the child is subject to the convenience of the system. Placement may be made in a foster home at some distance or, if no foster home is available, in an institution at an even greater distance. Since the parents are often poor and lack resources, contact between parents and child is thereafter limited. The treatment that the child's condition warrants may not be available in the parents' vicinity, resulting in the child being placed in an ostensibly better environment but at the expense of maintaining proximity and emotional ties with the natural parents.

Many social workers are uncertain about the role of the parents in the child's treatment plan. This is not surprising, since many of the children have unresolved conflicts with their parents. Since the parents are generally held to be the cause of the problem, and since preventive services to the family are limited, many workers find it difficult to justify maintaining bonds with the natural parents, especially if the family's problems do not appear to be remedied by the social services. This often results in cases where the child is retained in care indefinitely and unnecessarily because social workers don't recognize improvement in home situations when it occurs. In other cases, their hurried visits and susceptibility to parental pressure have resulted in cases where children *were* returned to unfit parents. The dilemma of whether to return the child remains a knotty enigma at the heart of placement decisions. Yet there is always great pressure to decide quickly, to ensure that the child does not end up "drifting" through the system while awaiting the resolution of his status within the natural family, for the longer the child remains in the limbo of the system, the more disruptive the intervention becomes.

Describing how the foster child feels about his placement in care, the Ontario Children's Aid Society report states that the child feels very positive about the way the home provides for him. He feels he is part of the foster family and that the foster home is his permanent place. In school, most respondents were one year behind their out-of-care peers; still, 85 percent of them stated that their goal was to go on to university. Fully 80 percent of the young people indicated that they found their social worker helpful, or very helpful, and only 19 percent found them unhelpful. On the whole, the children were happy to be helped by the service agencies.

This positively rosy picture is in glaring contrast to reports from the National Youth In Care Network — an association of young people in or formerly in care — and almost all other impartial studies that have compiled data on the needs of children in care. This discrepancy is not easily resolved. Brian Raychaba, who spent seven years in foster care and had what he considers an unusually amicable placement, points out that among his peers in the system he was an anomaly in that he desired to go on to university. "It was like telling some of them [other foster kids] that I was going to another planet. It wasn't that university didn't make sense or they had some other goal. It just didn't exist as an option." This should not be surprising, since higher education is the least of the priorities of a child in care.

Instead, it points to the unique viewpoint that the Ontario Society elicited from its respondents. The information cited by the Society report concerning educational goals, the feeling of permanence among long-term wards, and their positive assessment of social service providers is so out of touch with the actual attainments and feelings of youth in care that it casts doubt on the validity of its other findings. The report, which claims to be a blueprint for the future of foster care, does note elsewhere, anticipating almost certain disagreement with its findings, "that the [percentages] shown in this section are representative of the group only and should not be extended to the foster child population in general." But if the report does not speak for the "foster child population in general," how can it be a guide or blueprint for future development?

The pathos of the child in foster care can best be seen in the muted understatement of one child's response to the question "What do you most enjoy/not enjoy about living in your foster home?" The answer: "There is no radio with earphones and not enough video games. I'm told to play outside when I want to watch wrestling on TV." Then, tagged on at the end like an afterthought, but utterly to the point, "I'm not sure if I'm accepted and loved in my foster home."

A youth speaking with the author claimed to have been to seven homes in four years. He says he "escaped" at 16.

> I've been through hell. The only thing I done wrong was I didn't get along with my old man. We hate each other. So they send me to all these different places. In three of the places I was beat up by the men. One of the places was good, but I was moved from there after five months because this stupid worker thought I'd get something from this special program which was a lot of crap. The last place I was in, they were religious and I had to be in every day at 7:30, had to pray with them every morning, go to church, and all that stuff. They weren't bad people, but I couldn't stand the religious bullshit and I told them

one day just to stop feeding me all this shit. That was the end of that. Two weeks later I was gone.

Becky, 19 and recently out of care, cautioned against stereotyping foster parents.

> They're not all bad. A lot of them are really good. It's just that it's hard to get along with someone who's sorta your mother on a part-time basis. You know, it's hard for them, it's hard for you. I only had three sets of foster parents. I know a lot of kids who had more, way more. They were okay, but I can't say I was able to get close to any of them. It's not comfortable. I guess if you're lucky you can be friends, but they're really parents, you know, and it's hard for parents to be friends with kids."

Most youths, like the young man quoted above, speak of feeling unwanted and unloved. The cure, in a way, is so simple: make them feel wanted. But as a British Columbia commission seeking to understand and clarify issues in child welfare in that province concluded, "How does one legislate affection?"

The overwhelming consensus of the young people in custody is that the system of foster care does not provide a safe, nurturing alternative to their disturbed family life. They live in a world of rules and forms and regulations, which change from one home to another, one year to the next. Decisions are made for them by bureaucrats and committees with whom they have little contact. Frequently, the say nothing, for fear of retribution, or because it seems so futile: no one will listen.

The foster parent profile is as interesting as it is alarming. Although differences exist between rural and urban foster parents, by and large foster parents across the country are similar. They are recruited from the lower-middle class; the majority are over 40 and lack a high-school diploma. Approximately half of the foster parents have grade 10 or less. The father is a skilled blue-collar worker and the sole wage earner; the average annual income, exclusive of foster-home payments, is

$29,000 in Ontario (by comparison, in Saskatchewan the median is $19,000). That translates to approximately $12,000 less than the average income of Ontario households, even though, with the inclusion of foster children into their families, foster parents have almost three times as many children as the average Ontario family. The high age at which many foster parents take in their first child has been grounds for criticism of the system.

Church-affiliated organizations, especially fundamentalist Christian groups, privately own and operate networks of homes to which the state sends children. Many foster parents say that their religious background led them to consider foster care. Still more say they do it to see if they can help. Often they are recruited by friends and relatives. Only about 20 percent of foster parents sought out the possibility of fostering solely on their own initiative. The female head of the household, typically, is more involved in the day-to-day work of fostering.

Recruitment policies across Canada vary, but generally anyone who can supply the provincial or local agency with two character references, who has not been convicted of child abuse or molestation, and who can supply the basic necessities of food, clothing, and shelter can become a foster parent. This includes single parents as well. Training standards are virtually nonexistent, each agency providing its own extremely limited form of inhouse training for interested parents.

Nearly half the foster parents surveyed had not taken any training within a two-year period preceding the 1987 study in Ontario. This is in contrast to a 1980 survey, which indicated that more than half had never had any training at all. The 1987 report interpreted these results, incredibly, to mean that substantial improvement was evident in the attempts to train foster parents.

There was general ambivalence among parents about their role within the child welfare system. Over half saw themselves as professionals, but without the appropriate status and financial rewards. The remainder were split between maintaining the volunteer aspects of fostering so as to lessen the likelihood of "losing the family touch," and opting for a compromise status, somewhere between professional and volunteer.

When asked what the most rewarding aspects of fostering were, the majority cited the joy of interacting with the children themselves. However, they also noted that the fostering experience, despite their attachment to the children, was less than satisfactory. This resulted from a variety of factors, including perceived status, lack of incentives to improve skills, low financial reward, and lack of support from the various agencies. Nearly 70 percent asserted that social workers did not provide them with adequate information or assistance in dealing with their children.

Mirroring concerns in the general population, more than 50 percent of foster parents observed that allegations of sexual abuse and the method of investigating such allegations were cause for concern in their relationships with their children. Because of heightened public awareness of child sexual abuse, a child can now come forward with an allegation of sexual abuse and the child protection authorities must act on that allegation *as if it were true* until the investigation is completed. False allegations and the results of the investigations based on these allegation may be influencing the decision of many adults to foster. For those already fostering, much frustration centres on the issue of sexual-abuse allegations, as illustrated by the comments parents made when asked how they would like to see the system changed. They suggested:

> Making sure that nothing goes on record until all the facts are checked, obtaining legal support for parents, better all-round training for foster parents to teach them how to avoid being set up, taking special care in conducting allegations . . . and making sure children understand the consequence of false allegations.[6]

It would appear that as in society in general, there is a genuine fear among foster parents about the potential for and the consequences of false allegations and their limited ability to protect themselves before and during the legal proceedings following such allegations. The same complaint is made by teachers, daycare workers, and many others involved in child care, and it could prove to be a major stumbling block in the attempt by Canadian child welfare agencies to recruit more, and more skilled, foster parents.

On the other hand, the astonishing absence of comments by foster parents on the reality of sexual abuse for the young people coming into their care indicates that they do not understand the trauma for those who *have* suffered such maltreatment. If it is true that a higher percentage of youngsters, especially females, who come into care have been sexually abused, it follows that skill development in this area would be highly desirable, if the adolescents are to receive adequate treatment or understanding. Nonetheless, foster parents tend to focus upon the effect sexual-abuse investigations have on their own civil liberties.

But while no one likes to consider the possibility, a survey by Ross Dawson, the first of its kind in Ontario, suggests that the rate of physical and sexual abuse in foster homes is equal to or *greater* than in the general population. He suggests that in addition to sexual abuse as a reason for placement,

> the trend towards further deinstitutionalization of children will continue to increase the demands placed on the foster care system to accept and care for an increasingly difficult child population. That population is characterized by an increasing majority of adolescents, a growing number of children exhibiting emotional/behavioural problems, a sizable number of children who are present with behaviour which is dangerous to themselves or others. . . . These factors, combined with the higher level of scrutiny afforded to foster care by professionals and the public, and the trend towards increased awareness and recognition of abuse, suggest that without basic changes in the foster care system, a higher incidence of foster care abuse can be expected in the future.[7]

Confusion about the use of discipline is another concern across Canada. Many foster parents feel that they have to use two standards, one with their own children and one with the foster children. They are prohibited, by recent legislation, from using physical force as a means of punishment. Many parents, especially the men, were at a loss to understand how they would "teach the boy manners if you can't use the belt once in a while." This issue has not yet been clarified.

When foster care works or appears to work, despite an overburdened and underfinanced system and public indifference, it is clear that it can be extremely rewarding to those involved. One couple stated: "We believe in foster care. Nowhere can a child's needs be met more adequately than in a family setting. Children are the future of our nation. Their welfare is at stake. That is the responsibility of us all."

A second couple, who specialize in long-term care for the physically handicapped, wrote:

> Fostering has become a way of life with our family. The children in our care are our children, not by chance, but by choice. Foster parents cannot, nor ever will be, paid enough for all they do — the years, tears and joys are something so priceless that each one of us must give something of himself freely. Each family member's life has been deepened, strengthened and given true meaning of total commitment to other human beings through the act of fostering.[8]

Whether it is deeply felt religious conviction or a more secular humanitarianism that motivates parents, such satisfying experiences seem to be rare. Such recruits are scattered throughout the system, though it seems to be a matter of chance if they are matched with the kind of children they can effectively care for. Appropriate matches depend on the sensitivities of social workers, on their caseload, on court orders and backlogs within their area, and on the sheer impediments of the bureaucracy. The foster parents, like the kids themselves, often find themselves battling rather than applauding the system.

Foster parents go to great lengths to illustrate the division between themselves and the system they are a part of. They indicate that supportive case workers greatly increase the level of satisfaction they experience in fostering. However, they express ongoing dissatisfaction with what they perceive as a lack of respect from child welfare agencies, which have come to rely on them. Again, this suggests a contradiction at the heart of the system, a contradiction that explains why in many cases fostering doesn't work for the child or for the foster parent.

The majority of respondents in the Ontario report expressed frustration with the level of compensation. Some felt that receiving too much money would further darken their already tarnished public image, that they would be seen as taking in children for the money. Given the low rates of pay in all provinces it is highly unlikely that any of these parents are in it for purely economic reasons. Most felt that the pay was inadequate to meet the overall needs of the children in their care. In addition, such miserly incentives limited the number and kind of persons who would become foster parents and prevailed against their self-image.

The parents made numerous worthwhile suggestions about how to improve the fostering experience. These included co-operative stores where foster parents could purchase food, clothing, and other goods for their foster children, group insurance contracts for long-term placements that set out the terms and conditions of the placement, subsidized adoption for long-term crown wards, a multiple listing of foster children that would permit a preview of the children available to foster, and other such practices aimed at making fostering more predictable and more economical.

Perhaps the most important point to emerge from the survey is the finding of basic disagreement between the parents' conception of fostering and the agency's conception, for this leads us again to the question of what substitute parenting or caring consists of, in its essence. While many foster parents wanted simply to be like "mom and dad," they were expected to perform as professionals without any clear guidance or training towards that end. They suggested that due to the staggering caseloads carried by most social workers, they were expected to act as a liaison between the natural family and the child, implement long-term planning, and record and monitor behavioural management plans, thus spending time doing what they believe the agency should be doing and moving further away from what they wanted to be doing, which was spend time with their child. At the end of it all, despite their intense involvement in the day-to-day life of the child, they were excluded from the decision-making process. This increased the distance between them and the salaried professionals with whom they were working.

If compassionate persons from the community could be recruited to care for troubled youths, and if they were helped rather than hindered by the system of which they are an integral part, there would be no crisis in foster care. If they were paid professional salaries and given incentives to excel at their profession, and had critical input into the care and treatment of the children in their homes; if they participated in conferences with other foster parents and shared knowledge and training and new techniques; if they had well-edited journals rather than photocopied newsletters to keep them updated on developments in the field — if all these supports were built into the system, foster parents would become invaluable, satisfied participants in the work of healing as they were intended to be. Foster parents could then provide a reconstituted family setting in which a troubled child could reasonably expect to find both physical and emotional support. The unhappy reality, though, as evidenced by frustrations of both foster parents and their foster children, is that fostering is often a difficult and thankless task, without even an acknowledgment, in some cases, that the problems exist.

These compounded issues have led to a consensus among agencies and foster parent associations that voluntarism among foster parents is an anachronistic concept.

Foster parents across Canada are no longer satisfied with the system in which they play such a central but frustrating role. Patricia Melynchuk, a 28-year-old third-generation foster parent, explained how she felt that helping society's unwanted kids gave her a sense of helping the community at large. It was a moral duty she was taught by her mother and her grandmother. But after just two years and more than 20 children, it has become an overwhelming duty. Her grocery bills have tripled, she is continually scrubbing lice from the heads of her own children as well as from the foster children when they arrive, her house is a wreck, and the social workers from the agency "don't seem to give a damn about the problems." After her husband discussed with her the need for him to get a second job to cover the extra costs, she decided that it simply wasn't worth it. As with thousands of others across Canada, the high demands and the low compensation combined to destroy her commitment. She is turning instead to daycare. As she put it: "For foster care I get $14 a day, and for daycare I get more than double that, for an eight-hour day, and I don't have to supply all the other things that go with it, do the laundry, or bathe the children."

Ken Shaw, president of the Ontario Association of Foster Parents, estimates that the number of foster homes across Canada has dropped by half over the last five years, largely because the current generation of foster parents, who are the best recruiters of potential foster parents, are unwilling to seek out recruits. He points out that the issue of compensation, though relevant, must be seen in the overall context of fostering problems faced by the parents. Current rates, he says, have not kept up with inflation: the foster children today are older, more street-wise, and more difficult to discipline; the rising number of false allegations of abuse, the lack of pensions, the need for two incomes (which reduces the number of people capable of fostering), the inadequacy and the insensitivity of social workers, and the inordinate amount of time parents must take to make sure that everybody's rights are maintained — all these problems have made the job impossible to fulfil. His final comment, reflecting the cumulative dissatis-faction, is that foster parents feel that they are being exploited by governments as a cheap dumping ground for problem kids: "For less than 15 bucks a day the Ministry of Community and Social Services has gotten a free ride out of this."

Ontario Minister of Community and Social Services John Sweeney counters that Ontario expects to spend $29.6 million on the foster care system. He does not see how his ministry could justify higher spending. "By agreeing to the requests of the foster parents, including greater training and support, that budget would increase by about $9 million. I just don't have the dollars." It is also questionable whether pouring new money into an old system is worth the expenditure. The provin-cial government is waiting for its own report on foster care before responding to the parents. The minister, though, has speculated that small group homes may be necessary to handle the increase in the number of children with special needs com-ing into the system.

Throughout this continuing debate and the tedious task of clarification and seeking consensus, children and adolescents continue to suffer. It is they who are removed from their homes and placed with surrogate parents who for at least two decades have been festering with frustration that is only now being publicly acknowledged. Every year that true solutions are delayed results in another set of private tragedies as unloved children sink in the system.

If the behaviour of a child who is placed in foster care is not "normalized", if the major disciplinary problems cannot be corrected, the adolescent will begin his cascade further down the system: the next step is the residential treatment program reserved for more seriously disturbed children. There, with others equally disturbed, the youth will be subject to a variety of behaviour-modification programs intended to control or correct his defects. He will be judged by his performance in group therapy sessions. Where treatment is offered — staff are commonly reactive, rather than proactive — it is oriented towards behaviour management. There is little privacy. Doors are locked at night. A permanent undercurrent of resentment marks the relationships between staff and the young people. Failure to conform to the rules results in punishment specific to the rules and bylaws of the home: no allowance, further restrictions on their limited freedom, locked up in special rooms to "cool out", and so on. Physical punishment is no longer allowed in state-appointed group and residential treatment centres; psychological punishment, however, is pervasive and subtle. A 17-year-old youth commented:

> I was in three group homes. They're all the same. What staff is gonna know about you when they have to go home at three o'clock? They can go, right. But you can't. And what if you like someone and you want to talk 'cause you feel like this guy understands? They come across like that, like they care. They say, oh yeah, you can talk to me, but they're gone at three o'clock and what do you do then? Or what if you don't like someone, a staff or another kid, but all the time you gotta put up with them? If you don't put up with the kid, you get ploughed or you gonna plough them and if you don't like the staff guy, he gets all antsy and starts layin' heavies on ya. It don't matter, one place or the other, they're all the same, only some places are worse than others.[9]

An Ontario task force established to review group home procedures following the death of 21-year-old Krista Sepp — killed by two young males at a Toronto group home — concluded that seven of the nine facilities they investigated were overcrowded, had high staff turnover (some as high as 100 percent annually) resulting in part from low and inequitable salaries, had a shortage of staff, and the staff had little or no related training or experience prior to working in the homes.[10]

Adolescents who are removed from their homes are treated as if *they* had done something wrong. How else are they to perceive locked cupboards, small shared rooms, forced enclosure, and strict rules, all in the name of therapy directed by rotating shifts of inexperienced child care workers? How else do they interpret the evasive answers, the talk of courts and police and judges? If they were delinquent and confused when they came into the system, under these conditions they will remain equally or more troubled when they come out.

Residential treatment centres and group homes come in many different varieties. They are established to deal with a specific sub-population of the emotionally troubled youth referred to them by child protection agencies. They exist in cottage settings, "halfway" houses on residential streets, or as enclosed small institutions away from urban areas. Each staff-person is responsible for a number of children who have been judged unable to fit into the foster system. They work under the direction of a supervisor, either a psychologist, psychia-trist, or social worker. These workers, called primary care givers, need not have a university degree, although that is desir-able; they are usually young (between 21 and 28) and receive limited inhouse training. They spend an average of eight hours a day with the youths in their care on rotating shifts, guiding them according to the treatment program of their home. The more highly trained and better paid professional staff spend far more time planning, managing, and administering than actually working with the young people they have been trained to help.

The workers in these homes are generally the youngest within the child protection services. For these people, work in a group home is a foot in the social service career door, or an experiment; perhaps a first job, or a part-time adjunct to a university education. Qualifications vary widely. The constant tensions, the shift work, the heavy responsibility, combined with their meagre salaries and inexperience, leave them frus-trated, and they quickly burn out or move on to another type of social action. Transience among staff is accepted as an occupational hazard.

Residential homes represent a midpoint between the foster home and the last resort; it is one last chance before training school or reformatory. By the time children reach this stage, every arena is for them just another battleground on which they express their disenchantment. Their lives are filled with conflict and impermanence. Adults seem to have little effect influencing them to move in the direction of balanced emotional responses, enthusiasm for any task, or affection. The foster home, which had been envisioned as a place that could substitute for the natural home environment, failed. The stricter regimen of the group home has also failed. At this point, there is less attempt at socialization; the emphasis is on control, punishment, containment — not improvement of the *child* but protection of *society*.

This is not to say that the child care workers are bad. They are very likely the type of person the youths could relate to, but they are not given the chance to fulfil that role. The system is structured so that it offers no incentive to the group home staff to continue working within the group setting. There are limited career opportunities, limited use of their psychotherapeutic talents, limited positive feedback from professional colleagues, and a rate of pay less than half that of their professional counterparts. Next to foster parents, those who spend the most time with the children and upon whom the professionals rely for information, they are the least paid and the least trained to deal with troubled youth. Again, the ones who suffer the ill effects of this flawed system are the troubled youth.

It is a complex and fragmented world these troubled youth are thrown into. But while it is too complex and unsettling for a child to understand, it is equally discouraging for the administrators and front-line social workers of the child protection industry, who can, more than the child, see ahead to almost certain failure. Middle-class graduates of the nation's university or college programs, too inexperienced to deal with the tedium and tragedies they daily confront, and working in understaffed offices, are supposed to become the friends of these sensitive, disturbed young children. But neither their background nor their sojourn in academe have adequately prepared them for the life-altering decisions they must make.

The inability of the system to handle the bare logistics of the situation is illustrated by a case in Victoria, British Columbia. A number of teens came before Judge Loretta Chapman. She put one girl on probation for six months with the condition that she live where her social worker told her to live during that period. Her social worker suggested a particular teen shelter for homeless street kids, overlooking the shelter's inflexible three-day-limit policy; it had been established exclusively for homeless street kids. The girl's lawyer, Tim Leaden, attempted to get the worker to explain in more detail what the girl was expected to do for the next five months and 27 days of her probation order. The social worker was unable to answer. Judge Chapman, infuriated and confused, wondered aloud how it was that more and more of these kinds of illogical decisions were being made in her courtroom. Victoria, she said, was obviously not the place to be for a troubled child. Judge Chapman was unaware that this scenario is being played out across the country. The children, meanwhile, are stranded in a purgatory that seems more like hell.

Social work, for all its vaunted professional claims, is a dirty business. Not everything is rosy, and not everyone is saved. Bureaucrats, even the best intentioned, cannot tie up the multitude of loose ends. And so situations that are inherently the most "messy" — internal family problems and the murky issues underlying family breakdown — by the time they are summarized on paper and have percolated up to the top where the decisions are made, have little chance of being properly understood or accurately diagnosed.

Who are these social workers, and what are they saying?

The data we have, which again is limited, suggests that almost 70 percent are women. About half are married, and there is a tendency to move out of the profession when they have children, then return either full- or part-time. Most come out of four-year college or university programs. One-quarter go on to earn their Master of Social Work degree, gaining status within their profession. Nothing in their academic training adequately prepares them for the family violence they encounter in their day-to-day work.

Many say that they were not ready to admit that parents could be so cruel or that kids could be so vindictive. They quickly discovered that the system often didn't back them up or placed totally unreasonable demands upon them. One social worker put it this way: "Society expects us to be infallible. We aren't. We're just human beings. And we see too much to believe we have all the answers or even the right ones at the right moment."

Society's expectations put a great strain on the social worker. Directors and supervisors must enforce strict accountability for each step of the intervention process and enforcement of government-directed policies. Thus, the abundance of paperwork and the aims of social work as directed by government policy are often at odds with the social worker's ideal view of her profession. Social workers see themselves as agents of social change seeking and implementing social justice programs. For instance, one of the philosophic goals of social work is to plan preventive services that would lessen the number of family breakdowns. However, preventive work in Canada is not encouraged through either funding or legislation. Thus, the social worker is often involved solely in the "frontline" apprehension business, which is stressful and adversarial, or in attempting to coordinate badly developed and underfinanced in-care programs. The inordinate amount of time spent "pushing paper" leads many social workers to take on even more after-hours community projects, such as developing women's groups or self-help advocacy groups among marginal sectors of society in order to fill their true "vocation". This simply adds to the stress they already feel because of the conflicting roles they have to play.

But social workers do have a professional duty to be as thorough as possible in carrying out their mandate to protect the child and preserve the integrity of the family. And they have an awesome power. This statement by a member of the Ontario Association of Professional Social Workers who believes there are too few checks and balances within the child welfare system is representative.

> Anything can go wrong along the way and no one knows until the last moment, and by that time it may be too late. You always feel like you're in a management-by-crisis situation. And that doesn't help when it comes to making decisions. We have a lot of power that can be abused easily in the emotional situations we often find ourselves in the middle of. Parents are well aware of the power we have over them. We can say that we are going to remove the child to protect them unless they comply with our rules. That may be necessary to protect children from a lot of bad parents; however, every single parent who comes into contact with the Society, in my experience, is both afraid and intimidated by that power. Do you think they would be afraid of us if we were actually helping them?[11]

Perhaps the most stinging criticism levelled at social workers is one disputing or discrediting their training, which, it is alleged, leaves them ill-equipped to make the delicate, life-saving decisions required of them by society and their professional mandate.

Dr. Robert Seim, professor of psychology at the University of Waterloo, says, "I see the credentials of a vast number of social workers as having doubtful value if they lack a basic knowledge of child development. I see a system where too often the judge looks to the social worker for advice, and he or she does not have the creditials to do so."[12] Dr. Seim's criticism is echoed by Ottawa psychiatrist Selwyn Smith, who has bitterly attacked what he calls the ineptitude, poor judgment, and incompetence of the Society's front-line workers: "They make assessments of parents without the expertise to do so, return the child home and then we see the same child battered to

death. They have a tendency to play God without the wisdom."
Psychologist Robert Phelp puts it differently:

> You're dealing with an area which is neither a science
> nor an art when you talk about social work. Even at a
> Master's level, graduates become familiar with the intri-
> cacies of child welfare legislation, case studies of dys-
> functional families, and a hodgepodge of family
> dynamics theories. Are these graduates then capable of
> counselling and redirecting family dynamics, or asses-
> sing a family's psychosocial state? Are they capable of
> becoming good psychologists or psychiatrists, given
> their social work training? I tend to doubt it.[13]

All social workers involved in child advocacy pass through a
three-year B.A. program and a one- or two-year program
devoted to specific social-service issues. Course outlines
include work in deviant personalities, aspects of law as it per-
tains to child protection, a smattering of child- and adolescent-
development theories, and a variety of theoretical constructs
— such as sociobehavioural, ecological, or psychosocial theory — explaining causation in child and adolescent behaviour.

Following their university education, they accept positions
with a starting salary of approximately $30,000 a year. Out
among their colleagues, they learn on the job the kinds of
behaviour and diagnostic skills they are expected to exhibit.
Depending on the supervisors or other strong peers among her
colleagues, a social worker tends to interpret the behaviour of
children/adolescents in light of the dominant theoretical position of the agency. If she does not, her analysis or assessment is
countered by her more knowledgeable colleagues. Those who
fit continue with the particular agency; those who don't, go
elsewhere. There are sizable cliques within the social work
profession, each guarding their own way of organizing and
reacting to the behaviour of their clients. The particular school
of social work that new social workers gravitate towards will
determine how they predict and explain a client's behaviour,
how much change they believe can take place, and what tech-

niques and methods they will employ to induce the desired change.

Social workers adopt one of two major clusters of theory as the basis for intervention and treatment. For those who follow psychosocial theory as developed by Florence Hollis, the tendency is to view the individual primarily in Freudian terms: the personality is driven by the competing forces of id, ego, and superego. The social worker's primary role as an agent of society is to help the troubled child adapt to society by balancing the instinctual claims of id/ego against the moral claims of society, or the superego. According to the theory, the individual from birth is motivated by a set of drives derived from libidinal and aggressive instincts. Early experience is central to the formation of later character; generally, the individual's basic personality is formed by the time he reaches five years of age. Since the ego is often fragile in children who become their clients, the paramount concerns are assessing ego strength, developing a higher moral sense — strengthening the superego — and establishing appropriate treatment methods to help the ego adapt to the world. Frequently, adherents of this school of social work not only think this way but also speak this way.

Sociobehaviourists, the second major group, seek to change behaviour through positive and negative reinforcement, since that reflects their basic premise about human motivation as impelled by expectation of pleasant or unpleasant results. They rely primarily on conditioning techniques to establish or change behaviour. The focus is less on theoretical constructs than upon pragmatic means of altering habits, attitudes, or behaviour patterns.

A range of other theories falls between these two "classic" schools. Functional theorists, for instance, view individuals as having an inner force that motivates them to grow. The environment plays a key role in how orderly this inner-growth principle is allowed to work itself out. The social worker's role is to help individuals develop and channel their latent striving towards self-realization. Other, less accepted theories abound, but the point here is that the social worker leaving academia interposes a hypothetical construct between herself and the youths she is serving. Her training thereafter will consist of developing even more specialized knowledge in particular areas. With each passing year the social worker's cognitive framework is moulded by the paradigms of her profession, and she interprets the behaviours of the youths she meets accordingly. The theoretical crutch in time becomes the shield between her and the next new client sitting across the desk seeking help.

With their professional dress, demeanor, and theoretical background, coupled with their middle-class status and outlook, social workers are about as far removed from the life experience and status of their lower-class clientele as one could possibly get. Learning the essentials of their craft frequently consists of studying outlines of a series of casework manuals with instructions such as the following:

1 Core conditions of empathetic relationship building between client and helper in interview situations:
    a Appropriate and effective use of physical distance
    b Forward lean towards the client
    c Appropriately relaxed posture which communicates attentiveness, interest and concern
    d Regular eye contact with spontaneous eye movements
    e Fluid hand arm movements
    f Appropriate and alert arousal level which conveys involvement
    g use of appropriate face and head movements, e.g., affirmative head nods. . . . do not burst out laughing when client expresses sadness.[14]

Thus is the milk of human kindness diluted to an unpalatable broth.

Even should one learn by dint of dedication to "spontaneously" feel genuine compassion or empathy, such workers are a rarity among those who work closely with adolescents and their families. It is a rule of thumb among social workers that the more experienced you are, the further away from the front line you get. The most ambitious, or those with administrative talent or training, move away from the stress of front-line casework as soon as their qualifications are acceptable. Thus, the front-line worker, the one seen (or often *not* seen) by the child in care, is new and relatively inexperienced or else older, unpromoted, and burnt out.

Highly trained, experienced social workers tend to congregate in the urban centres rather than in rural areas. The closer one gets to major cities, the higher the socioeconomic background of the staff and the higher the level of university training. Salary scales in the northern child protection agencies are lower, so highly qualified personnel prefer to remain working in the metropolitan areas, where both the money and the standard of living are better. As one worker put it, "Northern Canada serves as a bleak training ground, a stepping stone to more plum appointments in the city. Once you've seen the squalor and filth out there, you want nothing more to do with that aspect of social work."[15]

The opinion among foster parents of professionals whom they work with varies: some credit them with being exceptionally dedicated and underappreciated, while others fault them with being utterly misguided in their fundamental approach to child and family services. A number of youths interviewed credited a social worker with helping them to get over particularly difficult periods during their time in care. A great number had either little good or else a lot of bad comments to make about the social worker's overall effect on their time in care. Among the low-income clients, who make up the bulk of the Society's practice, they are consistently seen as too powerful for their own good.

A parent who recently had his visiting privileges curtailed in the wake of a false sexual-abuse allegation was incensed by the social worker's "utter refusal" to see his side of the story.

They simply ignored my concerns and statements, preferring instead to believe my wife, who wanted custody of my child during divorce proceedings and accused me of child abuse. I couldn't believe the power they had over the context of my life and family relations. Later, when the whole thing was cleared up, I spoke with one of the workers about getting my name removed from the abuse register. She made it clear without actually stating it, that despite clear evidence to the contrary in family court, she still believed I had abused my daughter. And there was nothing I could do. They have a clause somewhere that these people can do whatever they want as long as they act in good faith. Well, if what they put me and my daughter through was in good faith, I would hate to see what they did to someone they didn't like.[16]

Other parents have voiced similar concerns, and all were very aware of the power of the Society to remove a child. Another parent said:

The officials of the Children's Aid Society are emphatic that it is the family court judge and not they who decides whether children are made wards. They deny the extent of their powers and the tremendous influence their recommendations have on the judge who can only make legal decisions, not deliver service. They exert enormous psychological, if not legal, power when they deal with families.[17]

Although their power and the possibility of misusing that power is formidable, the worker must also mediate and try to temper the effect of weaknesses within the system as they affect the child. If a child is going to need special care in a particular kind of foster or group home, and the social worker on the case knows that the home is full, this will affect her decision making and the mood and spirit in which she deals with the child. If she doubts the efficacy of sending a child to a home that doesn't match his needs, does she communicate her level of doubt or unease to the child? How does she feel about sending a scared young child into a first placement from which, she is reasonably assured, he will begin to drift through the system? Is the worker's doubt, or even guilt, in these cases, or her optimism in others, conveyed to the child, and how does that intangible pessimism in one case, or head start in another, affect the child's subsequent behaviour?

Social workers are saddled with the intricate bureaucracies of the system. They want to do good and feel justified in intervening, but the result of their intercession turns out often to be a grave betrayal of the child who placed his trust in them. The young girl's poem that began this chapter poignantly juxtaposes the intentions of the social worker against the emotional reality the child confronts. The social worker's reply is encapsulated in this lament from one who spoke bluntly and anonymously to the author:

> You're on the front line, you know everything that's going on. You've got mountains of paperwork before you even begin your day. You have a couple of priorities. Crown wards are low on the list. You hope they've been taken care of and that you only have to step in during crisis. So you go and see a family and you know that this kid is going to be dead or severely maltreated in his development because the mother isn't capable of providing even basic parental skills and the father is abusive. So you try and help her and she says "fuck you, child snatcher." Or you try to help, but there are a thousand and one things over which you have limited control and that get in the way of that attempted unification of the family.
>
> So you go to court using the child in some way to get to the family, to get them treated, you know, and still help the kid, 'cause in the end the kid is going to go back there. But you know nothing will change there and you keep your fingers crossed for the kid, believing maybe somewhere in this confusing process you can make a difference. But by the time you get to court, which is an adversarial system, and present damaging evidence against the family in order to save the kid, the family is

convinced that you are out to get them, which is true
enough in some cases, but you're really there seeing if
you can make any difference in this kid's life. You wonder if you should pursue termination of parental rights.
Then you've got more mountains of paperwork to justify every move you make and you have to live with the
gut knowledge that you don't have the resources or the
homes available. Maybe you should just leave the kid
there, but then what? It just goes on and on.

After a while you accept the flaws and just try to get
by. You rationalize. Sure, the system isn't the best, but
what can you do? It's neverending, the stress level, and
in the end who suffers? You know how many of my colleagues are leaving this profession? You know how many
of them are walking around out there completely burnt
out?[18]

It is the front-line worker, all too familiar with the under-
financing, the lack of resources, the happenstance method of
planning for the child's term in care, who must carry the load
of the Society into her daily struggle to assist her clients. It is
the social worker who must try to balance the prevention and
protection mandates of the child welfare system, who must
somehow "put the child's interest first" and at the same time
"seek to preserve the family at all costs" — often mutually
exclusive goals.

So while there is continuing talk of children's rights, of
prevention and unification rather than removal, and of limited
intervention, child removal or out-of-home placement occurs
ever more frequently. Provincial and federal funding is provided almost exclusively for out-of-home care. Funds have
never been available to back up specific programs that would
genuinely address the question of ameliorating abusive child-
rearing practices while allowing the child to stay *in* the parental
home, programs focusing, for example, on emergency, very
short-term shelter, daycare to assist overstressed mothers,

emergency cash assistance, homemakers' assistance, and intensive family therapy.

During the past decade the general dissatisfaction among children's aid workers with constant overwork and too many levels of management between them and the ultimate decision makers, has led to open conflict with management. Supervisors and directors of agencies themselves claim they, too, are overburdened with detail and financial matters.

John Pine got out of social work after a devastating experience he calls the "three solitudes." Pine had on his caseload an adolescent who was very demanding, but he specialized in handling such cases. He had worked closely with the foster parents to develop a stable base upon which the boy could work through his crisis periods. But there were built-in constraints in developing this kind of relationship. Since he was ultimately responsible for the boy, he couldn't allow the foster parents to make decisions that would affect the boy's volatile emotional state; therefore, they had to rely upon him, which diminished their sense of responsibility and control. They worked it out as best they could.

One time I was away for my holidays and a conference, about a week and a half. It's two days before I'm to go back. I get a call from my supervisor at work asking me about this kid. Apparently the kid's mother — he doesn't get along with her and she is a problem — is in hospital and the kid wants to go and see her. The foster parents tell him he has to wait to talk to me. I'm away. He's getting more and more pissed off. They phone the agency. The agency has been trying to get me for three days. I tell them the files are there and my backup knows about the case. But my backup is away too and it's the weekend and no one is around, etc., etc. By this time, nearly a week has gone by. The kid is furious. He's breaking things. He's threatening. He runs away. They send him to a juvenile centre. I say send him to the hospital, but send someone with him. I don't see why they didn't do this in the first place. They just kept putting the foster parents off.

Anyway, I suggest that he go with a worker and one of the foster parents for support. It's going to be arranged for the next day. Then I figure I should be there, so I decide to go in early. I'm pissed off because something so important to the kid has to depend upon me and not upon the foster parents, but what can I do? That's the way it's set up.

Just before I go in, I get an emergency call from the supervisor. The kid's mother died. He's going crazy. They had to call the police in. We never got that one straightened out. Not at all. The last time I heard, the kid was in a treatment centre for really disturbed kids. If he gets through that I'd be really surprised. That whole thing just floored me.

I went to see him, but what could I say — "I'm sorry I went on holiday? I'm sorry for the relationship you had with your mom that led to this kind of impossible decision-making process?" I couldn't say anything.

And in different ways you face that question every day. And I figured I'm one solitude living up as best as I can to my part of the mandate. The foster parents are another solitude, and the kid, he's the third and most reluctant part. All of us are working in and constrained by a system which we know is fucked up. But you tell me what to do. My answer was just to get out of it alto- gether and forget about trying to patch up the problems with bureaucratic band-aids. I just don't think it can work the way we've set it up.[19]

In his study done a decade ago, Peter Silverman reported that staff at the Ottawa Children's Aid Society demanded an inquiry into methods and practices of the agency. Five of the staff presented a petition to the minister of community and social services outlining their dissatisfaction, demanding an investigation into all Societies in Ontario, and recommending that they be abolished.[20] They stated, among other bold assertions, that while confidentiality was originally intended to protect the family, it was now used by the Society to cover up serious mistakes and instances of neglect or miscalculation. Nothing ever came of their charges.

Ten years later, Newfoundland's demoralized and disintegrating child protection authorities are reeling under charges of having "covered up" dozens of abuse allegations at Mount Cashel and in foster homes throughout the province. Ten years later, Native bands in Manitoba, only recently allowed to operate their own Native child welfare services, alleged that thousands of Native children were "kidnapped" by white social workers and sent out of the province to white foster homes and orphanages. Manitoba's child protection authorities originally denied the charges until proof of the claim was so overwhelming that one provincial court judge who investigated the practice branded it "cultural genocide" and put a stop to it in 1982. Then, in 1989, a young Ojibwa woman named Carla Williams flew to Manitoba from Holland with a nightmarish tale. She had been separated from her family for 17 years after being "kidnapped" and taken to Holland to live with her adoptive parents. The placement broke down after six months and she was sent to a series of orphanages, where she spent her childhood and early adolescence. She was sexually abused by her adopted father (she was sent home on weekends from the orphanage), bore two of his children, and ended up in a mental institution. After her emotional return to Manitoba, sponsored by Chief Louis Stevenson of the Peguis reserve, who also serves as chairman to the Anishnabai tribal welfare council, it was stated that a letter was sent by Dutch authorities to Manitoba officials explaining that Carla's placement had broken down. Janice Little, a spokesperson for the provincial family services department, denied that the government or the agency that arranged Carla's adoption had been aware of the breakdown. Little indicated that if they had known they would definitely have been involved. This was countered by Chief

Louis Stevenson, who had a copy of the letter sent by Dutch authorities to Manitoba officials informing them of the breakdown.

Not a lot has changed over the past ten years. With the incompetence of officials and the mishandling of client files, it is often difficult to get a clear picture of what goes on in the system of child welfare to which we entrust children. But it is clear from the wrecked lives whose stories surface during inquiries that the child protection agencies are comprised, it seems, of a wide spectrum of dissatisfied people. While the brunt of the criticism appears to be focused on the more visible front-line workers, and while for the most part the criticisms are accurate, what bedevils reformers and traditional child advocates alike is the intractability of the system. Only fundamental structural changes will remove the seemingly insurmountable problems that child welfare advocates confront daily.

The final ignominy is what happens when the system, literally as well as metaphorically, closes its doors on the children, now become young adults, as they finish their sojourn. Curiously, though there are many studies critical of institutional care, only a limited number of studies investigate the long-term effects of foster care on children. That limits the effectiveness of programs aimed at this population. What are social workers' ideas of success based on if they have no accumulated or comparative data showing what happens to children once they leave care? How do they formulate strategic programs aimed at youth leaving care? Apparently the child protection agencies have not seen this as a problem; the youth in care do.

Youths are no longer entitled to free state care once they turn 16 or 18 (depending on the province). They are given virtually no preparation; teenagers are turfed out of foster homes or so-called training centres expected to make their own way. Ill-prepared for their independence, many become dependent on other forms of state assistance, such as welfare. Their lack of education and technical skills leads many of them into stultifying and demeaning occupations. Their lack of social skills and work eventually precipitates a turn to crime. The John Howard Society reports that at least 75 percent of the inmates in Canada's institutions were known to child welfare authorities and that over 80 percent of this population were both abused during childhood and became wards of the state during their childhood or adolescence. Among this population, gross underachievement and low educational attainment are the norm. Gary Corbett, in an illuminating study, found that 90 percent of the street kids he interviewed in Calgary had been crown wards.[21]

Child protection agencies are still at it, perpetuating a system that routinely turns out uneducated, unemployable, confused, and isolated young people. Some of them, admittedly, do become successful. Some of them were matched with loving foster parents and refused to be cowed by their pre-care victimization. But youth in care, adult prison inmates, homeless youth, and a growing number of critics of the system tell us that successful foster care is more a matter of chance than of design.

What is needed are new ideas, completely new approaches to the notion of what these children are and what they are capable of. To remove them for their "protection" into a system that is itself demonstrably harmful (and largely unaccountable) is simply a more bureaucratized form of abuse.

Most children in state care need an incredible amount of time and emotional support from the adults within the system. Given the requisite amount and kind of care, most of these kids could eventually lead "normal", productive lives. But without an entirely new set of assumptions, they will remain locked in the premises of a failing system and continue to lose ground. At some point something snaps, a point of no return is passed, no life line can any longer reach the child. When a young person "loses the capacity" to form human relationships, he or she is irretrievably bound to a life of antagonism on the margins of society, unfulfilled himself and possibly harmful to others. A handbook for social workers pinpoints a crucial stage:

A foster child who moves many times, or who constantly fears that he may have to move, can suffer devastating effects. . . . He may become defensive, fearful, suspicious, and, after repeated moves, he may eventually protect himself from further disappointment and rejection by being less willing to invest in child-parent relationships. *Eventually he loses the capacity* [italics mine].[22]

Until the system of benevolence that has evolved over centuries to protect children attracts creative, compassionate program consultants and directs enough energy towards these cast-off children to provide them with a secure, stable, nurturant environment, they stand little chance of becoming anything more than the second-class citizens that they have been historically.

This is the crisis in foster care.

4

OUTSIDERS BY DESIGN: THE HISTORY OF BENEVOLENCE

"The Poor House? You refer then to the Poor House," said the secretary.

Mrs. Higden set that resolute old face of hers, and darkly nodded yes.

"You dislike the mention?"

"Dislike the mention?" answered the old woman. "Kill me sooner than take me there. Throw this pretty child I carry with me under cart-horse feet and a loaded wagon than take him there. Come to us and find us all a-dying, and set a light to us all where we lie, and let us all blaze away with the house into a heap of cinders, sooner than move a corpse of us there!"

Charles Dickens, *Our Mutual Friend*

Be it resolved that this conference urge its members to use their influence as widely as may be against the establishment or continuance of congregate institutions, and in those cases where it is naturally impossible to place all charges in foster homes or private boarding homes, members of this confer-

71

ence be urged to use their influence in favor of an
institution which will approximate as closely as
possible the normal home.

John Joseph Kelso, 1923

B enevolence towards children or their parents has never
rested easily in the political imagination of the Western
world. Dependent children, when regarded at all, have been
mute recipients of what adults thought was good for them.
Even the most cursory look at history shows how wrong we
now think some of those notions were. Still, exploring the
roots of our benevolent institutions establishes the context and
helps make sense of assumptions that, despite the good intentions of their benefactors, have oppressed dependent children
for centuries.

Our current notion of benevolence emerged directly out of
the early-seventeenth-century Elizabethan Poor Laws, whose
precepts migrated to Canada in the nineteenth century along
with the child subjects of those laws. But the Poor Laws as they
apply to children are rooted in a set of historical circumstances
that had prevailed in continental Europe since the early Middle
Ages. And although the circumstances have changed dramatically, certain attitudes remain, and they govern the way children of poor families are treated to this day.

In his illuminating study entitled *Madness and Civilization*,
Michel Foucault pointed out that the first monumental houses
of confinement were built across Europe to incarcerate and
separate lepers.[1] During the thirteenth century more than 2,000
leprosariums were spread through France alone — enormous
houses of confinement isolated from the rest of society. England and Scotland, following that lead, built 220 asylums in
remote areas to serve a population of just one and a half
million people. The leper, according to Foucault's analysis,
became the first systematically institutionalized "outsider" in
history. That practice was the precursor of the solution West-

ern society would use when dealing with people it could not tolerate for medical or psychological reasons.

The epidemic of leprosy that plagued Europe in late medieval times appeared to undergo "spontaneous remission": it all but disappeared. But in the burgeoning cities of the European trading nations, a new group of outcasts appeared, to take the place of the lepers. Originally, no one knew what to do with the unsightly, diseased, and dispossessed hordes of men, women, and children who left the countryside and roamed highways of the nascent mercantile world. One almost unbelievable solution was to put these "mad men and women, beggars all," to sea, a comic, pathetic cargo of lost souls. But even the infamous Ship of Fools, as it came to be known, had to dock eventually; thus, the deserted leprosariums found a second use, and history's second great class of outsiders appeared.

The Church responded to the waves of human impoverishment by creating equally large edifices to house the sick, the lame, the orphaned, and the invalid alongside these houses of confinement. But the number of the poor surpassed the Church's charitable intentions. Beggars became an affront to the more respectable, wealthy members of the rising middle class, and these upright citizens pressured their governments to do something about the crisis. In 1657 an edict was delivered in Paris aimed at that undifferentiated mass of people who had neither the economic means nor the social resources to better their state. Paragraph 9 of the edict read, "We expressly prohibit and forbid all persons of whatever breeding and birth, and whatever condition they may be . . . to be in the city of Paris . . . neither in the churches nor at the doors of such."

The king's guard would hunt down the beggars and hold them back at the gates of the city or march them off to the *hopital*, the name given to the old leprosariums. Across Europe, confinement became the preferred solution for vagrancy.

In England, whose laws the North American colonies later adapted, the problem of the poor was being given serious and profound thought at the same time that the Paris royal edicts surfaced. A pamphlet of 1622 tells succinctly of the way of life for the poor and the social problem they had become: "Though the number of the poor do daily increase, all things yet worketh for the worst in their behalf; ... many of these parishes turneth forth their poor ... to beg, filch and steal for their maintenance, so that the country is overrun with them."

The solution was found in the Poor Laws, which guaranteed able-bodied men a regular, unfluctuating rate of pay while the less able received a bare subsistence wage. The law had mixed motivation: it could be regarded as charitable in its intention, giving the desperately poor a pittance to subsist upon; but it was also exploitative of wage labourers and gave a man little motivation to work, since he could get the meagre "wage" whether or not he worked but could not improve his lot on that wage. Employers were disinclined to give more than the rates established by parliament forced them to give. Those truly unable to find work were prevented from asking for their guaranteed assistance by the stigma attached to the pauper and the odious condition attached to obtaining the government's handout. Men desperate enough to seek assistance, or refusing to work if able, were confined and forced to work in the workhouse or the poorhouse, as the houses of confinement had come to be called.

Throughout the eighteenth and well into the nineteenth century, the mood of the indigent rural populace darkened as the collective realization of their predicament grew. The poor were loathed and feared. Jeremy Bentham, a historian and political thinker of the period, was contracted by the English government to consider how the poorhouses could be maximized to house the poor, the insane, and others of the "lower orders." He suggested that existing poorhouses could be redesigned for multipurpose use, built to maximum efficiency, and spread proportionately across the countryside. Put the people into these workhouses and employ them usefully, productively, he said. Children, he proposed, could also play a crucial role in this employment scheme. He speculated that poorhouses could be governed in such a way that "indigenous" paupers would be conceived and brought up in them. Not knowing any other life, they would make excellent servants: industrious and servile.

Although Bentham's designs were rejected by parliament, some of his ideas were adopted in England and in the North American colonies. All manner of men, women, and children who were, for whatever reason, unable to support themselves were indiscriminately placed in the poorhouses. Later, as childhood became recognized as a distinct stage, children in need of special considerations not given to adult inmates would be separated and confined in orphan asylums. It can be conceded that for some sponsors of these asylums the intention was charitable, and undoubtedly many children were saved from starvation or other forms of fatal neglect, but this view must be balanced by the accusation that the cramped, often violent regimen in the orphanages caused many deaths, and life within them could not accurately be called anything other than a living death.

This was the nineteenth-century world Dickens wrote about, the world of Oliver Twist and Fagan and Betty Higden. The children of the poor wandered the city streets and the country roads "which they inhabit like rats" and from which they were taken by the authorities who enforced the Poor Laws. Hundreds of thousands of children escaped the lot of the poorhouse by being drafted "voluntarily" (if over 10 years of age) into the navy, or to be trained as apprentices and boarded out to the new lands, either Australia or North America. For the more sturdy of those who came to the unsettled land, it was indeed an opportunity to "make good," but the mass exodus of unfortunates from the "lower orders" also removed those who might "contaminate" the more virtuous working and leisure classes.

These children of the "juvenile immigration unit," as they were officially titled in the newly confederated Canada, largely go ignored and unmourned in the annals of North American history. The discussion about them that went on between various officials took absolutely no account of the children's expressed needs or desires. In fact, if their desires were considered at all, it was almost always with a view to how to eradicate or tame their "sinful" urges.

Philippe Ariès, a ground-breaking cultural historian, posits that Western culture "discovered" childhood during the late seventeenth century. Until then, according to his studies, childhood as a distinct developmental stage, requiring separation, protection, and education, was unknown. Children slept with their parents or other adults, were apprenticed at an early age (as early as eight or nine), and either were treated as chattel, almost as beasts of burden, when it was convenient to do so, or were considered simply miniature adults. There was no appreciation of the fragility and uniqueness of early stages of intellectual and emotional development.

The prevailing view of child and adolescent, however, underwent profound change from the seventeenth to the nineteenth century. The concept of childhood as a distinct stage took hold first and most clearly among the emerging middle classes of Europe. The Western nations were embarking on an era of industrial expansion that would need not only a large labour pool but also a smaller group of educated leaders and industrialists. The children of the middle class needed to be trained if they were to carry on the tradition. It was in this context that the public school systems gradually formed, freeing parents for daily toil and separating students who would eventually take their place according to their capacity and social status.

Dependent children, though, were in another class altogether. Considered "infected" by their parents' degenerate poverty, they were the last group to be affected by the gradual recognition of childhood as a distinct stage with attendant needs or a right to special care.

Aside from the industrial and commercial motivations to focus on the needs of childhood, religious and philosophical thought also affected the understanding of man, and of children. In many religious quarters, children were still viewed as unformed creatures tainted with original sin who had to be channelled into moral behaviour. The methods of training took various forms, from rote learning and recitation of Scripture, much as catechism was done until very recently, to a slightly more advanced form of education in Sunday school, where children were taught with methods that paralleled those being used in the developing public school system in England.

In other quarters, childhood was seen from a radically different perspective — as a state of grace and innocence, corrupted by the adult world, from which it should therefore be protected. This was represented in various ways in the influential teachings of people such as Mary Wollstonecraft and William Morris in England and Rudolf Steiner and Wilhelm von Humboldt in Germany. It was most lyrically presented in the literary works of Jean Jacques Rousseau. These two opposing strains of thought would converge awkwardly in a new type of children's institution, the orphan asylum. The asylums, while still grounded in a strictly disciplinarian mode of thought, went some way towards recognizing the special needs of children, and developed more appropriate pedagogical techniques.

By 1850 asylums had been established in most North American cities. They were designed primarily for the children of the "deserving poor." Those so labelled were able-bodied, but by force of circumstance were unable to participate in the work of building the good society. Children of the "deserving poor" were sent to the orphan asylums, where they were taught "useful" trades and received a modicum of education. The orphan asylum thus represented the first step in a political, institutionalized recognition and treatment of dependent children as children in need of protection, with programs aimed at preparing them to enter society even if only as servile and industrious members of the lower middle class.

Children of the *un*deserving poor, those of low moral character, or those who refused to participate in approved societal behaviours, remained in the poorhouses. Later, these less deserving would be placed in yet another version of institutional care, the House of Industry, the immediate forerunner to our reformatories, and just one step up from the poorhouse.

Rather than segregation and confinement with the purpose of educating, as in the orphan asylum, the emphasis in the House of Industry, then as now, was on punitive discipline and "reshaping" the personality. This was especially true of immigrant children, who, along with the offspring of "promiscuous single mothers" and other poor, outcast members of society, comprised the largest population of dependent and neglected children. They were treated not only as the authors of their own misfortune but also as the cause of problems in society. In keeping with the mood of the times, then Ontario premier Arthur S. Hardy responded to the child immigrant authorities that he intended to "guard against the moral or physical deterioration of our people" by refusing to allow immigrant children a place in the homes or institutions of Canada.[2]

These late-nineteenth-century responses to the problem of finding a place for needy children and the bitterness of the debates between enlightened thinkers and authoritarian theories can be understood only in light of earlier attitudes towards poverty and the immoral connotations it had, attitudes towards work as a ruling ethic throughout Anglo-American society, and wider socioeconomic developments. It takes only a short step back into history to discover that poverty and benevolence have gone hand in hand, that benevolence, indeed, often rests on the same premises that in other forms or manifestations underlie the conditions that caused poverty. It is clear, too, that during economic or political upheaval it is children of the poor, the most vulnerable, who suffer most.

Industry, unquestioning obedience, servility, and religious instruction was the main diet of children in orphanages. Without exception, the orphanages were poorly regulated and superintended. Every province in Canada had a poorhouse and an orphan asylum by the mid-nineteenth century. The poorhouses, like their counterparts on the Continent, were universally despised. Orphan asylums, though, had a mixed reception. Some felt they offered neglected children a chance they would not otherwise have had and at the very least saved them from the perils of the poorhouse. Contemporary critics talked of the "syphilitic pauper lying in his filthy bed" with nothing but daily drudgery to look forward to. When released at 14 or thereabouts, the children were indentured to a family who commonly paid little for what was in effect slave labour.

The orphan asylum would give way in time to the idea of the foster home, because it became obvious that the institution, however well intended, was too often a rigidly operated and unsanitary place, unfit for the habitation of children. Progressive child advocates, armed with theories from the new disciplines of psychology and sociology, argued that children's independence and energy were sapped by living in institutions to such an extent that they failed to function adequately in society. The institution fostered an unhealthy habit of dependence in the children, who would then, it was claimed, expect the state to continue to provide for them. It encouraged an inclination towards permanent dependency, which, in the new society that stressed rugged individualism, was not a welcome attribute. As the twentieth century progressed, questions of dependence, socialization, and emotional development would play a greater role in the discussion of child welfare.

The names of John Kelso and Charlotte Whitton stand out like beacons in the evolution of child welfare. These two Canadians heralded a change in approach that culminated in some of the better legislation governing child welfare today.

John Kelso almost single-handedly ushered in the era of professional social welfare in Canada. First as a crusading journalist and then as the executive director of Toronto's first Children's Aid Society, Kelso made passionate appeals on behalf of the poor. He was tireless and driven; he was also a product of a middle-class morality, which owed as much to its fear of pauperism and the "dangerous classes" as it did to compassion for destitute children.

In his 1910 report to the Children's Aid Society board of directors, he wrote:

The average poor family, we know, should not be con-
founded with that wretched class of people who seek to
live by charity and who have long since lost all pride,
self-respect or decency of conduct. . . . The aim should
be to restore them self-respect by steadfastly withholding
charitable aid and adopting drastic measures to force
them to self-exertion and support. For pauperism is
hereditary. Children are quick to learn that it is easier to
beg than to work and they grow up to continue the same
vicious, immoral life as their parents. Charity breeds
paupers, fosters and pampers them and inflicts upon the
community a long and ever-increasing succession of
degenerates to fill the brothel, the poor house and the
prison. Pauperism is a disease that can only be cured by
extermination.

Later he would justify the power of Society workers to investigate the lives of the poor with misguided paternalism and
thinly masked contempt:

Organized charity asks questions, but only in order that
it may give intelligent assistance. It is not like the police-
man who approaches you in a spirit of suspicion and
asks questions that he may convict, but rather like a
physician who must thoroughly reconcile, thoroughly
understand the ailment before he can effect a cure. . . . It
is safe to say, though, that the great bulk of those who
appeal for relief would have avoided the necessity for
such appeals had they been reasonably temperate, frugal
and thrifty.[3]

Kelso was imbued with a moral fervour and innate sense of
superiority with which he infused his workers when dealing
with the "lower orders."

For nearly three decades, from 1890 onwards, Kelso,
through his superintendency of the struggling Ontario-based
Children's Aid Society, and Charlotte Whitton, who rose to
prominence in the immensely successful Canadian Welfare

Council (previously named the Canadian Council on Child Welfare), fought to have children's homes carefully supervised, instituted casework methods of intervention, successfully challenged the idea that the institution or paid home — indenture — was a positive influence on children, and succeeded in replacing it with the free home or fostering ideal. Both Kelso and Whitton brought pressure to bear on governments to increase funding and to improve legislation governing child rescue. They sought and obtained the power to intervene in the lives of dependent children, whether in paid home situations or destitute families. They professionalized the social work services and in nearly all conceivable areas challenged and changed popular wisdom and practical realities of child rescue services.

By and large, Whitton's philosophical views, coupled with an increasing understanding of childhood development and a political climate permeated with a sense of rights and equality for all, still hold sway in child welfare departments across Canada. She envisioned that sentimental welfare based on public sympathy and philanthropy would be replaced by scientific welfare characterized by government-regulated agencies. Today, while one can criticize the implementation of child protection programs and the government's misplaced emphasis, the infrastructure of child and family services in Canada enshrines a conceptual understanding of children that still has the potential of liberating them from centuries of oppression.

Together, Whitton and Kelso mirrored the changes in society's views during the first half of this century. Like Charles Loring Brace, the founder of the first North American child protection agency, New York's Society for the Prevention of Cruelty to Children, Kelso was deeply moved by the plight of those without care or protection. "This great multitude of ignorant, untrained, passionate, irreligious children," he informed governments and philanthropists, "are potential members of the dangerous classes of the country." It was Brace who taught Kelso and other Canadians about the novel method of placing children in families, a system that had developed on the Continent. Against much opposition, Brace had transplanted thousands of children across the New York border into neighbouring Michigan to place them with willing families. The program's success, he declared, was remarkable. Kelso was impressed and followed his lead in Canada. "The family," he argued, "is the outcome of nature's own plan to secure the safety and growth of the child." To Brace and Kelso, as to most reformers, the argument for the free foster home was self-evident, and they pursued it with zeal.

In the first years of the Children's Aid Society, the main thrust was to professionalize and regulate the emerging child welfare system. But the Society's efforts were hampered by lack of funding, low salaries, competing ideologies, and fuzzy notions of its role. Many opponents still favoured the institutions the Society was fighting against or remained indifferent to its cause. And, while the social workers emphasized the need to rescue and protect children from morally corrupting or degrading physical conditions, they in fact apprehended children for a number of trite reasons, including trespassing on railway tracks, spitting on pavements, shooting pigeons, stealing brass from the CNR, unauthorized selling of newspapers, riding bicycles on sidewalks, drawing graffiti on alley walls, and playing ball in the street. Consequently, many people suspected their motives and feared their all-embracing authority. Their policies reflected a middle-class bias and incomprehension of the fact that poorer, lower-class families would engage in behaviour that for them was necessary and made sense; only to less needy people did that behaviour appear aberrant or criminal.

When the first children's aid society was founded in Toronto in 1891, it was regarded as a model child protection unit. By the mid-1920s nearly every province had its own society or government department dealing exclusively with child and family matters and operating with varying degrees of success. While Whitton attempted to regulate the entire range of services offered by the nation's child protection agencies, she was less able, working at a national level, to directly affect or change the prevailing practices in local agencies. What she was able to do was to set the standard by which child welfare regulation could be judged. That few lived up to the standards was a reflection on them, not on her proposals. Patricia Rooke points out,

When one examines the results of the Canadian Council on Child Welfare surveys conducted in New Brunswick, various centres in Ontario, British Columbia, Nova Scotia, as well as commissions of inquiry in Manitoba and Alberta from 1927 to 1947 . . . [one will observe that] uniformly the CASs . . . were identified as weak links in the realization of professional and "scientific" child care.[4]

Each Society operated according to its province's child protection act. From the earliest days of these organizations, some of the main problems that would later impede them were already apparent. Most were underfinanced, staffed by inadequately trained workers, and had to continually fight public apathy or outright hostility. Furthermore, the inherent difficulties of the situation — putting children who were already problematic together in a closed environment — coupled with inadequate supervision of the children and workers, created an atmosphere in which the lowest common denominator would prevail. It was inevitable that abuse within the Society's centres would occur. Finally, one other problem that to this day bedevils social intervention agencies of many types was evident: the insolvable problem of judging humans, of predicting their potential, of labelling and categorizing them and upon that basis assigning them to one regimen or another from which they almost certainly emerge as examples of self-fulfilling prophecies. The Societies failed to distinguish between dependents who were simply neglected and destitute and in need of special care and those who were truly delinquent and posed a danger to society.

In 1928 John Mills, director of the Toronto Society and a tireless and outspoken crusader for the free foster home ideal, had only three paid staff working on family and casework in a city that listed a population of 255,000. By the time he retired in 1947, the Ontario Society had grown to a staff of 88, with an annual budget in excess of $700,000, and it handled over 5,000 cases a year. Towards the end of Mills's tenure, the orphan asylum as a method of treating and educating children had given way to the fostering idea as espoused by Kelso. By 1940 most asylums acted only as clearing houses for children in need of shelter or as homes for handicapped children who were previously considered unplaceable.

Thus the institution first inhabited in medieval times by lepers, then by madmen and the poor, became in time the place for all dependent children, until it too passed the burden of benevolence over to the government and the emerging professional class of social workers, to retain, in its most modern version, only those children with extreme needs that cannot be met in any other setting.

Ironically, the demise of the institution was brought about by what Mills would have complained was the desire of governments and funding bodies to get child welfare "on the cheap." Fostering as an ideal caught on not because the government was persuaded that it was inherently better than the largely unregulated boarding-out practices and orphanages it replaced, but because in the end, fostering was economically more feasible. Yet the problems seemed to move as well from one method of care to the other. Today fostering, according to child care advocates, is in jeopardy of failing for the very same reasons: because the government is still trying to get child welfare on the cheap, and because lack of training and poor regulation and supervision are destroying the effectiveness of the foster home system.

Charlotte Whitton in 1940, in her report to the Canadian Welfare Council on the conditions of child welfare in the provinces, could say:

It is a sobering reflection that Section XIX of the Elizabethan Poor Law of 1601 provided that "this Act shall endure no longer than the end of the next session of parliament." It would doubtless be as surprising to the members of Elizabeth's parliament as it is to many Canadians that many of the actual provisions of those early Poor Laws and many of the social and political ideas which lay behind them, had endured into the middle of the twentieth century.[5]

Yet even Whitton, probably the single most important champion of dependent children, had second thoughts and in later years regarded her efforts at centralization as finally destructive of community-based charity. She criticized the bureaucratization of child welfare, fearing, correctly it now seems, that such efforts would ultimately impersonalize the service social workers were attempting to provide. She asserted in 1949, on the eve of her resignation, that "the centralization of child welfare was a threat to individual liberty and a sure route to state welfarism." Nonetheless, the initiatives that she helped to originate would evolve into a new paradigm of child-saving programs incorporating formalized expertise, certification, advanced training, standards of ethics and regulatory procedures, and cumbersome welfare bureaucracies, and would include in its professional ranks social workers, pediatricians, psychologists, diagnosticians, parole and probation officers, juvenile court judges, and family counsellors.

By the first decade of the twentieth century the child savers had recognized that by preserving and reconstructing the family unit the number of dependent and neglected children would be reduced, and their rallying cry evolved from "save the child" to "save the family." Even that quantum leap in the understanding of how problems arise and how better to solve them could not overcome government stinginess. The great majority of foster children have, and still do, come from among the poor.

In 1968 N.H. Lithwick, in a report commissioned by the federal government, stated:

The poor are not seen and, being out of sight, are out of mind. They live near the core of large cities or in rural backwaters where most of society never goes. Many of them do not shop at the major grocery or department stores. They do not lie on park benches, at least not many of them, and those that do are not representative of the hidden poor to whom I am referring. They attempt to get by, to feed themselves and their family. To send them to school. To participate in the opportunities presented to all North Americans. They have the same desperate need to succeed as the rest of us, but lack significant resources.[6]

The poor in Canada, unlike the poor in some other countries, know that they are a distinct minority. They see all around them the wealth and status that they are denied. This is especially true of the growing ranks of working poor. As described by a member of the Family Bureau of Greater Winnipeg:

For the working poor, who comprise by far the largest poverty group, the lack of income is not the most dramatic criterion for poverty. Rather the lack of opportunity, resources, and power are the more significant concerns. Life needs, such as shelter, food, and clothing are somehow meagerly met; but such luxuries as recreation, and supplemental purchasing power, do not often exist. Poverty lines don't effectively describe the true nature of poverty; nor do any of the other often-used social, economic, and political criteria define what it means to exist at a subsistence level.

Our communities are not geared to supporting low income people who lack purchasing power or social influence. If an individual admits defeat, our society benevolently places him on welfare, and he faces bureaucratic control of his activities. His life is then governed by the rules and principles of an often archaic system, which believes a person on welfare relinquishes his rights. Also, he must not be allowed to become too comfortable for fear that he will become a parasite.[7]

Because so many of the children in care come from households below the poverty line, and because so many foster homes to which they are sent are themselves just above the poverty line and therefore unable to relieve the effects of poverty in the children's lives, it is worthwhile to look closely at the issue of poverty. The difficult idea for the non-poor middle-class person to understand is that 65 percent of the poor are working poor. That is, they work at minimum-wage jobs but are unable to feed or clothe their families adequately. Among this class of people the work ethic simply hasn't paid off. And among the rural poor, the disappearance of many small communities and the erosion of the extended family means that whereas it was once considered "easier" to be poor in the country than in the city, even there, today, poverty becomes unbearable.

The poverty of Native cultures is far too complex to explain fully here, but they, among the poor we are considering, exemplify most starkly the assumptions of misguided benevolence.

There is no question that among the poor, the Native people are the poorest. Whether status or non-status, whether on the reserve or searching for a place in the white man's world, they are victims of poor education and health services, which comes down to poor housing and sanitation. Behind the paucity of services to them stands the malignant racial stereotype that fetters them. With their culture decimated by the whites and their future unsettled, many depend almost entirely on the benevolence of the white man who destroyed them. Their children are the most helpless of all victims in Canada, and it is these children who make up the largest percentage per capita of children in care.

In an address to the Alberta government, representatives of the Métis Society, articulating the thoughts of many Native people, had this to say about poverty:

Basically, poverty among the Métis is simply a lack of
employment and adequate incomes. However, there are

secondary aspects of poverty, such as housing, colonial-
ism, racism, and cultural circumstance. For those born
into poverty, no enrichment of the mind can be accumulated; awareness of racial or cultural identity cannot
grow; and there is almost no hope for the expression of
individual potential. Instead disease, insecurity, hunger,
cold, injustice, harassment, and oppression prevail. There
is little opportunity in any avenue, and practically no
incentive to develop the mind and the spirit. People who
are born in poverty learn to think, feel, and act so that
not only do they adapt themselves to living in poverty, but
[they] restrict themselves to performing in that particular
environment. Furthermore, they are unable to learn how
to think, act, and feel in a way that will permit them to
function adequately in a non-poverty environment.[8]

These thoughts were repeated by the white poor whose pleas
for understanding illustrate that poverty, whatever its cause
and whoever its victim, is universally destructive:

To become poor, to be forced to seek welfare assistance,
is to be damned to second-class citizenship, to be
thought of and treated as something less than a human
being. Raped of dignity, you experience constant panic,
frustration, deprivations and injustices. Worse still is the
shattering hopelessness of knowing you are trapped . . .
because the system is designed to keep you there . . . to
maintain you in the welfare trap. . . . Unless you possess
extraordinary determination and good health, or are
blessed with good luck, you will remain trapped on welfare street, to stink and die there.[9]

John Colletti of the St. Vincent de Paul Society in Halifax,
an organization that deals with a wide spectrum of society's
marginal classes, says: "Intervention, in the form of an ill-
assorted and uncoordinated series of welfare measures, not
only failed to provide the desired, lasting solution, but brought

about the conditions described by all as the mess of the Canadian welfare system."

No one speaks well of the welfare system we now have. In that sense it is not controversial: everybody is against it. Why should this be so, given the enormous sums of money we spend on it? An answer emerges from a description of the system and how it operates. The inadequacies of this social assistance program parallel the problems faced by its sister, the child welfare organization: too large, too impersonal, too bureaucratic, not controlled by those most directly affected. Good intentions notwithstanding, neither of these monolithic systems is providing anywhere near the level or quality of services that is feasible. As one member of a government commission on poverty in Manitoba put it:

> An adequate attack on poverty is not simply a matter of providing some sufficient income . . . but is very much a question of the manner or process by which such a sufficient income is provided. If its provision is seen as an act of benevolence, even though it is the impersonal benevolence of the state, it will support the largely false assumption that poverty is the fault of the poor, and will reinforce the feeling of recipients that they have no right of their own and no control over their own lives. Their well-being depends on others. There develops a state of helplessness, powerlessness, alienation and cynicism.[10]

The question revolves around whether income maintenance is a right or a gift. The traditional answer has been to consider it a gift. The system was set up so that the worthy poor would be discovered by an investigation, would receive resources, and would be "helped" through a variety of welfare rehabilitation programs to use those resources properly. The fact, though, as we can see looking back on four or five decades of the welfare society — indeed, looking back on four or five *centuries* — is that governments have tended to give enough social assistance to keep people alive — that is, to keep them there — but not enough to boost them to a higher rung on the socioeconomic ladder. The problems of ghettoized poverty — powerlessness, cynicism, narrowed vision, despair — are clearly perpetuated from generation to generation.

Between 80 and 90 percent of the nation's dependent children come from the ranks of the welfare population or from among the working poor. Approximately 30 percent of single mothers give up their children for brief periods in order to get ahead, making that incalculable parental sacrifice for the benefit of their kids, whom they feel will stand a better chance in the state's child welfare system. Many more have their children removed against their will because they are unable to provide the children with secure homes. The children did nothing wrong. They are not being punished. If the state could assure the children that it had a better alternative, that it was going to become the parent they never had and nurture independence, productivity, and hope, then the cycle of poverty and despair that dwarfed their lives would come to a stop. But in the end one has to conclude that the state is failing to provide a viable alternative, failing the children just as it is failing their parents. Somewhere in the child's frail psyche, this deprivation is registered as punishment; punishment for something he did not do. The effects of this scapegoating are what we see years later when the child comes out the other end of the system and, more often than not, acts out against society the crimes for which he has already paid.

Despite acknowledgments of our lack of progress over the decades, there have been some major conceptual advances regarding the status of children. Society has come to see childhood as an important stage in human development when the child needs the "room" to develop, and to which all children have a right. While this is not yet apparent in practice, it is honoured in policy. The United Nations Declaration of the Rights of the Child, Principle Two, nobly proclaims:

The child shall enjoy protection, and shall be given opportunities and facilities, by law and by other means, to enable him to develop physically, mentally, morally, spiritually, and socially in a healthy and normal environment and in a condition of freedom and dignity. In the enactment of laws for this purpose, the best interests of the child shall be the paramount consideration.

Principle Six opts for a less utopian but still lofty ideal:

The child, for the full and harmonious development of his personality, needs love and understanding. He shall, wherever possible, grow up in the care and under the responsibility of his parents, and, in any case, in an atmosphere of affection and of moral and material security.

These profound sentiments reveal the changes that have taken place in the conception of childhood over the course of six centuries. However, if the United Nations Declaration is held up as a standard against which the child welfare system in practice is to be judged, the system is clearly seen to be a dismal failure. As Charlotte Whitton understood years ago, making practice match policy must become our most energetically pursued goal.

5

MODERN INTERVENTION

*It is a paramount objective [of the Society] to pro-
mote the best interests, protection and wellbeing of
children. . . . The protection of children, including
responses to complaints of child abuse, has always
been and continues to be a priority in the services
offered by . . . [the] Society.*

Introduction to an Ontario urban agency
service manual

Riding the tidal wave of public concern about child abuse
generally, and child sexual abuse specifically, the government has rushed to the rescue of children. This is good. But in
their haste to deal with the once hidden problem of child abuse,
the public, the politicians, and the policy makers have over-
reacted. Countless programs have come into existence over the
last decade in a nation-wide expansion of child protection
services. These programs seek to protect all children in the least
possible danger of future maltreatment. They even attempt to
treat all those who were abused in the distant past. Through a
combination of federal laws and statutes, agency policies, and
public pronouncements, the idea has been fostered that all
children coming to the attention of the authorities are auto-
matically protected from future abuse, and, additionally, that

if children *not* removed from their homes are subsequently injured, a child protection agent must be at fault. Consequently, child welfare professionals are now so fearful of letting a child remain in a potentially abusive environment that they intervene in family matters on the merest suspicion of abuse. The law sanctions and the public applauds the intent and sincerity of their efforts on behalf of abused children.

We now acknowledge that many parents and legal guardians abuse their children physically, sexually, and emotionally. Since children are powerless to defend themselves, the state has an obligation to protect them, much as an older brother would protect a younger sibling, or a loving parent a child. But a question remains. Can the needs of a child for love, affection, guidance, and training be translated into a system of rules and regulations? We can *protect* a child by removing him from an abusive situation, but can we *care* for him? This is the dilemma facing child welfare apologists across Canada, who recognize that child welfare as it is deployed today is failing to meet the needs of much of its clientele.

Over the past decade, all provinces have reported a 500 to 1,000 percent increase in the number of abuse allegations and a concomitant rise in the number of investigations. This has led, on the one hand, to the state's ability to identify a greater number of abused children. On the other hand, by overextending the limited budget and resources of agencies, it has hampered their efforts to deal effectively with the increasing number of young people requiring out-of-home placement and treatment. It has also led to a heated and often contentious debate on the merits of state intervention.

While all parties involved — the public, the politicians, and the child protection services — agree that the interests of the child are paramount, they also agree that a balance must be struck between the need to protect children, the availability of resources to carry out this task, and the protection of civil liberties of families. There is not yet enough research to tell us clearly to what degree child welfare agencies are failing, but in the area of substitute care, child protection agents are suffering from what can only be termed a crisis of faith. This crisis affects foster parents, child protection agencies, and government funding.

Philip Hepworth, a pioneering Canadian child welfare researcher, concluded a study on apprehension and prevention by suggesting that multiple contradictions are besetting the child welfare services, and he suggested "rethinking the philosophy on which child welfare is based." Hepworth was concerned primarily with the lack of resources, with the fact that, barring an expanded social support system that recognizes and responds appropriately to the needs of the poor, child protection services will remain necessary but ineffective.[1] Hepworth and his more activist colleagues, such as David Cruikshank, professor and associate dean of the faculty of law at the University of Calgary, are clear about the solution. Prevention rather than apprehension, they argue, may be the only effective course. And yet preventive services are unlikely to develop, given the historical unwillingness of governments to address the underlying causes of poverty and economic disparity among child welfare clients.

In response to some very probing questions at the time, the British Columbia Royal Commission on Family and Children's Law was established in 1974, under the chairmanship of Mr. Justice Thomas Berger. It evolved in the end into a "complete examination of child welfare throughout Canada," sparking debate in the reform-minded child advocate movement of the seventies and leading ultimately to legislative changes based on its recommendations.

The crucial issue guiding the Berger Commission was the question of state intervention in the lives of dependent people. When the law perceives people as dependent, it usually endows a guardian appointed by the state with substantial powers over their lives. Women used to be treated this way. Native people still are. And so are children. But children are a special class of dependent. If the family cannot care for the child, or if the family unit breaks down, the law allows the state to intervene and assign the child to parent substitutes. These may be foster parents, adoptive parents, group homes, or institutions. There are cases, the Berger Commission posited, where all would agree that a child should be placed in a substitute setting. (Such a case is examined in this chapter.) But there are an equal number of cases where all would disagree with each other. At what point and by whose standards should the care that parents are providing to their child be measured?

To answer these and other tough questions, the Berger Commission first spelt out the most basic needs of children — among them clothing, shelter, warmth, affection, emotional security, mental health, and education — and went on to recommend that these needs should be interpreted as rights and be legislated accordingly. They sought then to refine their discussion of these points. Do children have a right to a permanent home, or to adequate services within their home, or a specific level of care and treatment? Can we presume to legislate affection? When can the state presume to override the family's right to privacy, a right enshrined in the Charter of Rights and Freedoms, to be subverted only for compelling reasons?

These far-reaching questions carry us into the current debate about children in crisis situations. Until the Berger Commission published its conclusions in 1985, there were no Canadian textbooks on child welfare policy and practice; Canadian schools and other human-services teaching units relied exclusively on U.S. publications. Even then, the commission found that Canadian child rights activists agreed on very few points. Three fundamental issues are the focus of dissension: What is the status of children as members of the state? What are the appropriate divisions of responsibility between state and parents as the stewards of children? And how can parents and children be best motivated to carry out their responsibilities? Social activists assume that an implicit pact exists between the state and the family, the breaking of which by either party elicits a response from the other. The purpose of the British Columbia commission was to analyze the assumptions of this implicit pact and to suggest which alternative among possible responses to a broken pact was best.

It is interesting to note here that as insightful and far-ranging as the Berger Commission's recommendations were, it neglected to deal with the obligations of the state once a child had been removed. For instance, it did not ask how the state can be best motivated to carry out its responsibilities. This omission is common among researchers and reformers of child welfare.

In Canada, civil libertarians believe that however important the care and protection of children is, it is not the proper business of the state. Parents, they claim, have the primary responsibility for meeting the basic needs of their children, although health and education concerns are shared by them and the state. According to this view, the child welfare system should intervene only when the life of the child is threatened or the level of care is well below community standards.

All Canadian government-funded child welfare services follow this "residual" model. They ensure child safety and provide alternative care where necessary, including limited in-home services during a crisis period, which bolster the capacity of parents to care for their children. The federal Canada Assistance Plan, which cost-shares social-service programs with the provinces, is a direct example of the residual model. Under this plan, family allowance, child tax credits, and deductions for children, child care, and substitute care are approved by the federal government to assist families in the care of their children. The government assumes that the individual is capable of and responsible for carrying out his civic duties, including caring for his children, with minimum government assistance. The government intervenes only during crisis or breakdown of the family.[2]

A second, more radical view holds that because the state is ultimately dependent on the child — as a member of the next generation — it becomes responsible for more than the child's safety. In this model more than the first, children are viewed as a vulnerable group with special needs and rights. Within this framework, society's understanding of what constitutes the needs of a child should be incorporated into its "social utilities programs," bringing child welfare up into the range of the broader economic, educational, housing, health, and social-welfare policies. The residual view is rejected because it philosophically justifies government's limited crisis-driven role in providing preventive services to children and families. Thus, while child advocates struggle with minimal success to ensure children and families the right to expanded in-home services such as homemaker, emergency cash, or subsidization, the pragmatic realities of child welfare have for the most part followed upon the premises of the residual model. And because the government adheres to this crisis-driven model, Hepworth and his colleagues concluded that preventive child and family services are unlikely to ever evolve.

Such are the opposing positions of progressive agencies and social activists and of conservative governments. And they directly affect the criteria used to justify differing levels of intervention, levels represented at either extreme by interventionists and non-interventionists. Non-interventionists invoke the "best interests of the child" principle as a guide for courts and other decision makers. In order to remove a child from his home, the child protection agency would have to show clear and compelling evidence that the child's life is threatened and, in addition, that the state has a long-term treatment plan that guarantees permanency. Since the state cannot guarantee permanency in most cases, it should intervene only when the danger to the child clearly calls for apprehension. Non-interventionists argue for a more extensive preventive-service orientation, which would support the parents before family breakdown occurred and the need to apprehend the child arose. In the end, the non-interventionists are saying that given the uncertainties of life within the state care system, its limited resources, and the psychological needs of the child, apprehension of the child should be a measure of last resort.

As a final criticism, non-interventionists point out that the system of checks and balances breaks down when the state replaces the natural parent. When a child is in his natural home, representatives of the state act as back-up supervisors or guardians, to ensure the child's wellbeing. But when the state itself becomes the primary guardian, there is no one left to supervise or double check on its performance.

Interventionists, on the other hand, focus on the potential benefits of state intervention in any dysfunctional family. They dismiss the concerns of non-interventionists as retrogressive. All children, they argue, deserve a chance to improve their family life either within or outside their family home. Since the state has alternative homes for children with willing substitute parents, then the state has an obligation to remove children from negligent families and provide them with the opportunity to lead significantly healthier, more fulfilling lives. If the parents are non-compliant, the children should be removed. Both views tend to be invoked in different aspects of current legislation. But in the author's view, the non-interventionist position more clearly recognizes the fundamental difficulties with state intervention.

Of the ten provinces, only Ontario has statutes pertaining directly to preventive services. In other provinces, funding is earmarked specifically in terms of the residual model, which responds only to crisis and thus limits the kinds of intervention an agency can employ. As authors Alfred Kahn and Sheila Kamerman put it, "The issue is not whether the government will intervene. It will. The question is whether it will intervene for enhancement and prevention, or whether it will respond to breakdown, problems, and deviance alone."[3]

It is difficult but necessary to untangle the network of good intentions that have nevertheless created a badly skewed intervention procedure. Child protection must absolutely remain an item of highest priority — abuse should never be allowed to be secreted again as it has been historically — but we must be on guard against a government that, under the banner of benevolence, sanctions wholesale interventionary tactics, undermines civil liberties, and potentially harms both the children and the adults it intends to help.

To see where law and statute, social worker and agency, and the public meet in this complex dynamic, it would be instructive to follow the modus operandi of a social worker involved in a typical abuse investigation, from initial contact to final decision in family court. (The case is based closely on real events, though the names have been changed to protect anonymity.) Bear in mind that while the general format outlined here is true for most agencies and government-appointed child protection workers, there would be particular differences, depending upon an agency's specific policies.

On January 15, 1989, at 11:30 A.M., Sandra Donaldson, a public school teacher at a large downtown school, is toying with the telephone in the teachers' lounge, trying to decide whether to call the local child protection office. She has discussed her concerns confidentially with a colleague, but still she hesitates. If she does not call, but suspects abuse, she is liable to a $1,000 fine. But more than that, the sexual-abuse educational programs she has seen recently have deeply affected her. She hadn't known the telltale signs of abuse or what abuse did to an otherwise innocent child. But after viewing the programs she couldn't help but note as she scanned the classroom that a number of her grade six students were exhibiting behaviour that could have suggested sexual abuse.

As Sandra sits nervously by the phone, she is thinking specifically of Donna, a formerly active 10-year-old who had, over the course of the year, become more withdrawn, arrived at school early and left late, and who lately had been falling behind with her schoolwork. A colleague had told her that Donna sometimes posed suggestively in the presence of boys during phys. ed. classes. Sandra had tried to talk with Donna, but had been unsuccessful. She didn't know what to say. How could she ask the girl if she was being abused? Some of the signs were there, but what if she was wrong? Then again, what if she was right?

What pushed her to making the call on this particular morning was a conversation she had had with a neighbour and classmate of Donna's, who told Sandra, in response to discreet questions about Donna's situation, "that her dad's always drunk and her mum's a wreck. Donna talks to my mum about it sometimes." The classmate hadn't said much else and Sandra didn't want to probe. She made the phone call.

The intake worker handling the phones at the agency was reassuring. He took down the particulars and told Sandra that they would be in touch with her shortly. Following standard agency procedure, he then called his supervisor and alerted him that a suspicion of abuse had been filed with the agency. After gathering all the details, the supervisor noted that the education programs in the schools were definitely working, a fact he was relaying with satisfaction in the upcoming annual report. There had been an 80 percent increase in reports of suspected abuse, especially from the downtown schools. The intake worker checked the assignment roster: Elaine Smith was scheduled to take the next case.

Shortly after lunch, Elaine was informed of the allegation. She checked the file to see what needed to be done before interviewing the young girl. By law, she would have to interview the child within 12 hours of receiving the report. Often, that wasn't enough time to get all the particulars, and she preferred to have as much information as possible before talking to the child. She had the name, address, and telephone number of the allegedly abused child. The girl's last name, Bellany, rang a bell, but she wasn't sure. She would have to check the Central Abuse Register. She had the first names of the parents, knew there was one other child in the home, and she also had a brief profile of the teacher who had reported the abuse. There wasn't much to go on, really. Under the law, she had 24 hours to complete the dossier and three days to cross-check and confirm all identifying information concerning the alleged abuse and enter it into the agency's centralized record. But first, she had to see the child.

By two o'clock, after shuffling her caseload — she carried 28 active files — she called Sandra Donaldson. She confirmed the particulars and attempted to clarify Sandra's concerns. She agreed that the psychological signs — the early arrival and late departure, the gradual withdrawal over the course of the year, and the decreasing interest in schoolwork — did signify cause for concern. Sandra wasn't sure, she explained to Elaine, if Donna was actually suggestive, as the phys. ed. teacher had reported, but she would talk with her again. Elaine asked about Donna's brother. Sandra informed her that the brother had graduated from grade eight the year before and, yes, he did seem to have a number of difficulties, but she didn't know too much about him. Elaine wondered if Sandra would introduce her to Donna. She also asked Sandra to write her concerns out so that she could have a written record of her suspicions, as agency protocol dictated.

At 3:15, just before school let out for the day, Sandra Donaldson called Donna aside and informed her that she was worried about her deteriorating school performance and other things, and wanted to know if she could help in any way. Donna was non-committal. A short time later, Elaine arrived. After introductions, Elaine explained to Donna who she was and gently explained in more detail the teacher's concerns. She wanted Donna to know that if she needed assistance or if her family needed assistance, she could arrange certain things. She would just like to help in any way she could, Elaine said.

Sandra observed that Donna, though initially uncomfortable, responded to Elaine. She began speaking of home and hinted that it was difficult there. Her brother often picked on her, she said. And her father was always away. He'd come home late, she said, and though she didn't state it directly there were intimations of alcohol abuse. Donna said very little about her mother. Elaine asked if she was picked on by anyone else in the family — cousins, say, or uncles or grandparents. Again, Donna was vague. At this point Elaine asked if she had suffered from any of a number of diseases or if she had ever had their symptoms, which she then listed. She got the name of Donna's family doctor.

Elaine asked Donna if she had seen the film *Good Touch — Bad Touch*, which was about undesirable sexuality. The film had recently been shown at all downtown schools. Donna said that she had seen it. Had anyone ever touched her in ways that she didn't like, in ways that the film had suggested were bad touch? At first Donna didn't answer. She looked at the ground, began fidgeting with the corner of her dress, and mumbled something. Elaine asked again. Donna nodded and said that someone "had touched her bad once." Elaine and Sandra exchanged knowing glances. It was true. Someone, most likely in Donna's family, was sexually abusing her. Is anyone touching you like that now, here at school or at your home? Donna shook her head no. Donna seemed uncomfortable and relieved at the same time. Elaine offered to give her a ride home.

Before leaving, Elaine told Sandra that she would be recommending a more detailed investigation, and she thanked Sandra for responding to the signs of abuse, which, although ambiguous, were often of just this kind. Sexual abuse, she said, as much as we wanted to dismiss it, was happening with increasing frequency and was not restricted to any one social class.

On the ride home Elaine explained more elaborately to Donna what a child protection agency was and that if there was anything Donna felt she needed, Elaine would try to help her. She could sense that she had gained the girl's confidence. She explained to Donna that sometimes bad things happen to us and we want them to stop, but it's hard to know where to turn. She wanted her to know that no matter what, Donna could turn to her. Elaine said that she would also like to speak with Donna's parents, and left her with her number at work and an emergency number where she could be reached if anything came up and Donna felt the need to talk.

Elaine returned to the office, uncertain about whether Donna would be safe in the house, and decided to push for an immediate investigation. She checked to see if the family had shown up on her or other agencies' listings. There was nothing. Nor was the Bellany name listed on the Central Abuse Register, a list of names of alleged and convicted abusers compiled by

the child protection services throughout the province. Her conversation with the family doctor would require a release of
information form, which she couldn't get without parental
consent, and that, too, would have to wait until her discussions
with the supervisor and abuse investigation team. Although
Donna had said that she was not being abused at this time, that
might have been said out of fear or embarrassment. But
whether she was or was not currently being abused, one thing
was clear: she needed help. And besides, Elaine had a gut
feeling that the abuse was continuing. She stated as much in
her written report to the supervisor, dropped it off, and left for
home.

The following morning Elaine elected to visit the family.
Donna's mother agreed, reluctantly, to meet when her husband
returned around one o'clock. After hanging up, Elaine
reviewed the case. It was not clear who or when someone had
sexually abused Donna; certainly, her school performance and
withdrawal from activity suggested that with or without sexual
abuse she was unquestionably "failing to thrive," a catch-all
term that presupposes a significant degree of parental neglect.
Perhaps Elaine could offer assistance to the mother, enrolling
her in a homemaking or parenting-skills course. However, she
knew that the few programs there were had long waiting lists,
and she wasn't sure how effective they were. In any case, she was
more worried about the child than about the parents at this
point.

When Elaine had told the mother that the Society had
received a complaint and that she was investigating to see if she
could help in any way, the mother was immediately defensive
with a trace of hostility. What right did she have coming in and
telling them what to do . . . and so on. Protect the child and
enhance the integrity of the family — the two never quite
seemed to work in tandem.

Since the investigation depended upon her investigatory
skills, she had to establish a good working rapport with the
family, despite the difficulties. And she had to resolve, in a
limited amount of time, whether the child was being abused

according to the standard definitions of abuse found in the
Child and Family Service Act, namely:

1. That the child has suffered physical harm, inflicted by
the person having charge of the child or caused by that
person's failure to care and provide for or supervise and
protect the child adequately.
2. That there is a substantial risk that the child will suffer or may suffer or may likely suffer abuse which the
parent or person having charge of the child caused to be
inflicted. . . .
3. That the child has been sexually molested or sexually
exploited by the person having charge of the child or by
another person where the person having charge of the
child knows or should know of the possibility of sexual
molestation or sexual exploitation and fails to protect
the child. . . .
4. That the child has suffered emotional harm, demonstrated by severe anxiety or depression or withdrawal or
self-destructive or aggressive behaviour and the child's
parent or the person having charge of the child does not
provide or is unable or unwilling to consent to services
or treatment to remedy or alleviate the harm.[4]

The meeting with Joan and Dan Bellany was tense. Elaine
explained again that the agency had received a complaint and
that she was investigating. They wanted to know who had filed
the complaint. Elaine refused to identify the informant but
reiterated that it involved their daughter and that the Society
had been asked to help. She noted that Donna looked a bit sick
and that her school performance was slipping.

"Ah, she just never eats," Dan replied testily, "and she's a
lazy cow. She don't do nothin' around the house either." Dan
did most of the talking, only turning to seek confirmation
from the mother. Elaine listened, noting the dreary, run-down
appearance of the house, and the liquor bottles stacked alongside the fridge. She inquired into their health, occupations
(Dan was an unemployed seasonal worker), number of other

children living at home, problems encountered, agencies or community services involved, and so on. She persuaded a reluctant Dan Bellany to sign the doctor's release of information form.

Elaine spent two hours that afternoon with Donna, walking, talking about her home and the problems with her assertive father. He had occasionally beat her; more often he just ignored or yelled at her. He frequently beat her brother. Her mother did nothing, otherwise her father threatened her too. Donna admitted that she wasn't happy and felt helpless. Gradually they came round to the sexual abuse. Donna became vague and uncertain. Finally she blurted out that her father had sometimes come into her room and molested her. He was always drunk, and he would warn her not to say anything. He had not yet penetrated her, although she thought he had tried once. Suddenly she began crying and denied it was true. "I made it all up," she kept repeating, while Elaine comforted her.

It was a classic form of disclosure, which Elaine had heard many times. The pain and confusion, the reluctance to admit, and then the pent-up hurt rushing out like a dam bursting; then the recantation. It was described in the sexual-abuse literature as the "post-sexual abuse accommodation syndrome." Elaine expected that Donna would shift back and forth over the next few days, admitting one moment, recanting the next, feeling betrayed, feeling that she herself was the betrayer and hoping that someone could help her. Could she help? Having brought Donna this far, where could she take her?

From here on the formidable, relentless machinery of the state would come to bear on this girl's life, and Elaine herself could do little to change its direction. It would fall to her to explain to Donna that she did not have to go home, or more specifically, following the guidelines set out in the Child and Family Service Act pertaining to sexual abuse, that she could not *allow* her to go home. How would her parents react, and more importantly, how would Donna respond to this displacement? Elaine knew that this was the end of one nightmare but could be the beginning of another.

Elaine took Donna back to the agency. She informed her supervisor of the disclosure and allegations and made arrangements with a colleague to set up emergency placement. She telephoned the Bellanys to inform them of their daughter's allegations and that Donna did not want to see them at this time. The Bellanys denied everything. They demanded to see a lawyer. Elaine informed them that there were no active criminal complaints at this time, that the Society was only interested in protecting Donna from further abuse and, if possible, helping the family to resolve this problem. Donna would be placed in a "safe" home until the matter was settled.

Donna now depended heavily upon Elaine. But she had paperwork to do and placement arrangements to make. Someone else sat with Donna while Elaine continued with the practical details. Later that evening Elaine dropped Donna off at an emergency foster home run by Beth Mitchum. Beth was discreet, gentle, and understanding, the kind of person Donna would need over the next few days as the investigation gathered momentum. Elaine remained at the home till late in the evening, comforting a distraught Donna.

The following morning Elaine's supervisor advised her that they had been receiving irate calls from the family. It seemed that they were not going to be compliant with the investigation. He had already alerted the abuse investigation team, who were working on a 21-day management plan to cover the court hearings and placement plans for the young girl. He reminded Elaine that time was of the essence in collecting and recording in writing all relevant reports from professionals involved with the family and rounding up any potential witnesses.

Elaine was glad that she had seen Donna before the girl had gone home. If the parents had refused access while their daughter was under investigation, she would have had to request the police to obtain a warrant to enter the premises to search for and apprehend her.

She continued the step-by-step investigation process that determines the decision of the court. It was up to her to marshal all the available facts and present them to the court in such a way that the judge could decide, on the "balance of probabilities," the disposition of the case.

The next question was whether Donna would be required to testify in court. Many times children become fearful and refuse to testify against their abuser when they have to face him or her. New rulings allow the judge to use discretion in deciding whether the abused and the alleged abuser will have to face one another. Elaine would suggest an audio-video recording of Donna's allegation. Judge Roquet, the county's family court judge, was fairly compliant in this regard. Finally, Elaine contacted Sandra at the school to warn her that she may have to stand as a witness during the proceedings.

Accompanied by a male social worker, she visited the Bellany home to explain the legal procedure the agency was obligated to pursue following such allegations. She explained the family's legal rights in the upcoming family court hearing that would determine their daughter's immediate future. It would be best, she suggested, to admit to the accusation and perhaps find a way to resolve this problem. If they admitted to the abuse and sought counselling with the agency, the disposition would be more favourable. Both parents adamantly denied the accusation. Elaine indicated that if abuse, sexual or otherwise, were determined by the court to have happened in fact and was likely to happen again, the court could, depending on the severity and duration of the alleged abuse, allow the child to remain at home under agency supervision; could remove the child into temporary wardship with limited parental access, during which time both child and family, separately and together, would undergo counselling; could remove the child for an indefinite period with no parental access; or could terminate parental rights altogether, making the child a full ward of the state. The decision depended at this point on their compliance with the agency and their attempts to resolve this issue. Dan Bellany said that they would fight. Before leaving, Elaine observed the living quarters closely, visited Donna's bedroom, said she wanted to talk with their son, and discreetly received clothing and personal items for Donna from Mrs. Bellany.

From the time of disclosure to the videotaping session one week later, during which Donna Bellany recounted many incidents of sexual abuse at the hands of her father, the girl saw and related her story to a psychiatrist, a psychologist, a medical specialist, the police, two social workers, and a foster mother. Her father refused to have anything to do with her. Eleven days later, the court, based on the evidence and on the non-compliance of the parents, terminated parental rights, making Donna one of the 12,000 Canadian children who each year enter the labyrinthine world of child protection. Within three weeks, Elaine introduced Donna to Marilyn, a social worker who would be taking over her case. Elaine told her not to worry, that people were around who would help her now.

Because there was a shortage of specialized treatment programs available to children and young teens suffering sexual abuse, Donna was moved from the emergency foster home in one county to a foster home in another, 40 miles away, in order to take part in a program that had been started there earlier in the year. Elaine attempted to keep up with the girl's progress, but her time was taken up with the increasing number of girls like Donna who came to the attention of the authorities in much the same way. The agency needed her investigatory skills more and more, cutting down her complement of routine cases. Gradually, she lost touch with Donna.

Donna did not attend school during the two weeks it took to make her a permanent ward of the state, was sent to a different school for one week while they sought a permanent placement, was then transferred to another foster home in another region, and to another school, when it was determined that the treatment offered there outweighed the need for consistency or continuance in education. Two months after her initial contact with the agency, she was living in her second foster home with two other foster children, an older and a younger girl. Her case review noted that permanent plans were difficult to arrange and that although she was making progress in her treatment program, she had not come to terms with the abuse. School performance was deteriorating, and the foster mother com-

plained that the "balance" in the house had been "disrupted."
She could not say that this was Donna's fault, but the transi-
tion had not been an easy one for either Donna, who was
depressed, or the other girls. The mother would wait and see
what happened during the three-month trial period before
commenting further.

Donna's new social worker, Marilyn, visited once a week to
help her deal with the abrupt transitions in her life. She noted
in her reports that she thought it would take time for Donna
"to come to terms with the sexual abuse and disturbed family
relations by which she has been severely traumatized." It is
expected, she said, that when a permanent arrangement can be
found (which will be difficult, given the reluctance of foster
parents to accept children older than five), Donna will be
moved again to a new foster home, which will mean a new
school and probably a new social worker. If no permanent
substitute arrangement can be found, or if Donna becomes
even more depressed, she will likely be moved to a number of
foster homes before "settling in," or failing that to a psychiatric ward or residential treatment centre for intensive psycho-
therapy.

Donna's brother refuses to speak with her. She has no contact with former friends, as she is separated from them by
nearly 50 miles. She has no desire to make new friends while
she is adjusting to the abrupt changes and uncertainties in her
life; thus she is basically alone. She finds it difficult to speak to
the counsellor at the treatment program because she isn't sure
if "something else will happen to me if I say anything else."

Donna's future is clouded. There is no statute governing the
type, duration, or level of effectiveness of treatment programs.
There is no statute governing the number of homes or schools to
which a child should be subject. There is no measure against
which the agency's actions could be judged emotionally abusive.
There is no definition of "systems" abuse. Whether she will be
helped to deal with the alleged sexual abuse or the cumulative
negative emotional effects of displacement following her disclo-

sure is difficult to say. The law is concerned only with her apprehension. After that, despite the best intentions of her teacher and social worker, she is abandoned to a series of recommendations that depend on the capricious resources of the child protection system. What happened to Donna and the uncertainty surrounding what will happen to her in the future is precisely what happens to many apprehended children.

I have deliberately chosen a case where everyone would agree that the child was in a dangerous, abusive situation. But in many cases, it is unclear whether the parents are abusive according to the vaguely worded definitions of abuse, "failing to thrive." In such situations, the Society's ability to assemble a case against a parent dwarfs the ability of a parent to mount a defence against the state, especially when the agency has the ability to almost reshape the historical events that form the basis for the termination. Cultural and class biases of agency workers can affect the shaping or re-creation of that history. But what happens after the child is removed is an open question. The state is very involved with identifying symptoms, but it has little to say regarding the "cure".

Michael Hartrick, an expert on child law, explains some of the dynamics of these situations.

> The events in the case unfold in the context described by the agency. It may be that services are wanting or inappropriate; caseloads are high; agency efforts assume certain capabilities of the parents; those capabilities do not exist; administrative necessity strains effective relations; prejudices of agency officials abound; visits with children become infrequent due to strained relations with the agency; contact with agency personnel becomes sporadic due to mutual mounting frustration.
>
> Then all attention turns to the children. The children enjoy the attention. They begin to drift away from the parents who are seen to be in a continuous state of anxiety. Former problems with the parents are magnified during this period. The parents may at some point rec-

ognize they have to change to suit the agency's definition of compliance, but by this time the agency will no longer consider additional assistance [to the parents]. That was attempted. That was history. And the history as the agency presents it to the judge will convince the judge that the parent is non-compliant.

For the parent, there is little to deny and the best explanations sound hollow when compared to the "best interest of the child." Thus the parent is defeated by a history of failed visits, past failures, misunderstanding, inadequate housing, or whatever the original unsolved social problem was that brought the agency out to them in the first place. And then, then you remove the children for a length of time to be determined by the judge and supervised by the agency, which is involved in an adversarial relationship with the parent. The agency has the power at this point to say if you do not comply you lose your kids. And justice or child protection is seen to have taken place because the attempt at reunification failed and the parents were seen to be the cause of that failure. It is very complex. It is very hard to find truth among these issues.[5]

There is no perfect solution. The Berger Commission, struggling with these questions, recommended that when government exercises its "state as parent" role it should act as follows:

Before the courts even become entitled to hear a case for intervention, there should be statutory protection which reflects a new doctrine of *parens patrie* [state as parent].

The developing doctrine could be termed the family support theory of state intervention. It holds that no compulsory intervention by the courts should be permitted unless the family has first been offered supportive services in the home. Furthermore, in the event that services are refused or would clearly be late and inadequate, the neglect finding of the court should always be tested against the available disposition and resources. If the child cannot get a proper placement through the child care agency, the finding of neglect notwithstanding, the child should be returned to the parents.[6]

This sane and reasonable directive attempts to convert aspects of child welfare philosophy into legislative and practical reality. As a directive, it illustrates the determination of progressive non-interventionists to limit the state's intrusion into family life, while balancing the needs of vulnerable and abused children.

Over the course of a century, haphazard service delivery, intrusive and traumatic intervention, and inappropriate placements have remained constant in child welfare circles. We understand the need for limited intervention, both on a practical level, in terms of available resources, and on a political level, in terms of civil liberties. What remains is to overcome the successive failure of child protection agencies and provincial governments to implement their more enlightened understanding of developing children. That success would, at last, be truly in the best interests of the child.

6

RICHARD CARDINAL: A CASE STUDY

I was friendless, alone, and very scared. They said I'll get over it. My new foster parents took me to the place I was going to stay in their house. They took me down the steps into a basement covered with water. There is one 40 watt light bulb. It doesn't have anything over it. It looks like something you see in a horror movie. . . . I kept telling myself that this was all a dream, that I would wake up with my brother Charlie and my sister Linda. . . . But I knew it was not a dream, that I was going to wake up and be right here. It was then that I began to think about suicide.

From the diary of Richard Cardinal

On June 26, 1984, 18-year-old Richard Cardinal was found hanging from a tree outside his sixteenth foster home. His foster father, John Crother, had gone searching for him in the usual places Richard wandered to outside the expansive farmhouse. It was a hot, muggy day. Richard was nowhere in sight. His foster mother checked with friends. John Crother eventually spotted Richard hanging by a rope from a board in the tree that he had told them he was going to use for chinups.

Mr. Crother raced back to the house, informed his wife, and phoned the police. He reluctantly took photographs before the

115

police arrived, stating later that he wanted people to see what he had seen if there were ever going to be people who needed to talk about what went on.

As the police cars sped through the streets of Sangudo, Alberta, word raced through the community that a young Métis boy had been killed. Few recognized the name. Richard hadn't been there long enough to get to know anyone. He had been with the Crothers less than two months. Some said he had killed himself, but nobody knew for certain. It was possible; Métis were an unpredictable breed.

The police stayed with the Crothers for five hours, investigating, taking tests, talking to the foster parents and anyone else who could shed light on Richard's suicide. For two hours his body hung there, bloated, silhouetted against the barn. They were still waiting for the coroner to arrive when someone decided they should cut the body down.

After learning that no further forensic procedures were necessary, the police constable placed the body in a morgue bag, tagged it, expressed his regrets to the Crothers, and drove back into town. No autopsy was performed.

"We kind of figured that the social workers would want to know what had happened, but they just had us collect his stuff and said they'd be talking to us," said John Crother, a serious, slow-talking, amiable man who had only briefly known his foster child before the suicide.

In the week after Richard's death there was much activity in the Northwestern Division of Alberta's Social Service Department. A social worker who had been working with Richard for six weeks since his transfer to Sangudo arranged the funeral on her own initiative. Richard's six siblings, his natural mother, the Crothers, and a few social service staff attended.

But as the weeks went by almost everyone except the Crothers seemed to forget about Richard. "We waited the week out, figuring everyone would be tied up with the funeral, and then two weeks, three weeks, and finally I just said to my wife that this wasn't right. They got to do something." The Crothers wanted to know what had gone wrong. Why hadn't someone fully informed them of the boy's past or why hadn't someone spotted the boy's distress? Maybe they could have done something if they had known.

One month after Richard's death, John Crother sent the photographs he had taken of the body hanging from the tree to several provincial ministers and child welfare supervisors, asking why there was no inquiry. Suddenly, there was a flurry of activity. Journalists from Edmonton got wind of the story and began investigating. People were interviewed, an inquiry was called, and slowly the agonizing story of this sad, sensitive boy was revealed to a chastened group of bureaucrats and officials. His death had become a reproach to the soulless labyrinth of the child protection system.

Richard Cardinal kept a diary of his time in care that, alongside the official "progress" reports of his numerous social workers and foster parents, chronicles his tour of the system and almost inevitable slide into suicide. There is conflicting evidence as to who persuaded him to write a diary. One of his foster mothers said she did, but Richard dedicated the book to "my brother Charlie who inspired me to wright [*sic*] this book."

Richard was born on October 7, 1966, to Métis parents. He was the third-youngest in a family of seven children. He was apprehended one day short of his fourth birthday. A social worker had found Richard and his two younger sisters in their home in the company of an inebriated, semiconscious man. There was no heat in the house, the children's hair was speckled with lice; Richard had open sores on his head. Their mother could not be found. He was moved to a foster home in Fort McMurray; his two sisters were sent elsewhere. Richard was described as being an active, happy, four-year-old boy. Less than two months later, when it was learned that the foster mother suffered from an undisclosed medical difficulty, Richard was moved to another foster home not far away. Eleven days later, after the second foster mother broke her arm, Richard was moved again.

He remained in his third foster home for nine months. He

had no contact with his natural parents and only occasional contact with his brothers and sisters, who were placed in a series of foster homes in and around Fort McMurray. His social workers' and foster parents' reports indicate that Richard at this time was still a "happy, healthy, active young boy," although he was having trouble "accepting authority." Charlie, his older brother, whom Richard saw occasionally and who was arguably the only person he loved and was loved by during his brief life, alleged that Richard was often beaten by his foster parents for minor infractions, a common experience for both him and Richard.

Between March 1972 and February 1973, Richard was moved to three foster homes, none of which was suitable. The social worker involved discovered that one family was leaving on vacation and not taking Richard with them. The social worker began to "question this family's commitment to Richard" and ultimately had him moved three times before finally finding a "suitable" place for him and his brother in the town of Lac La Biche. Richard was not yet seven years old.

Charlie describes the beatings he and Richard were subject to at this home.

> We would do something, like anything, and the old man would be waiting for us. He had this big stick and he'd have us take our pants down and then he beat us. He used to get the family, three girls and two boys, to come watch. They'd just be standing there and we'd have our pants down and we'd get beaten. We were both glad to get out of there. It wasn't a good home.

They were sent to the nearby town of Breynat. Over the course of the next year they were sent to two more foster homes. In his diary Richard wrote:

> I returned to school this year. I am glad because I was not considered an outcast like before. . . . I had my first taste of puppy love with a girl in my class. It felt good. I wanted to be there all the time. . . . But then a social

worker came and asks me how long it will take for me to
get ready to move. I said about a week. I should have
said never because now I had to leave again.

In the next home Richard was accompanied by his brother
and one sister. It was the happiest time of his disturbed young
life. Nonetheless, progress reports indicate that he had become
more impulsive, difficult to handle, and his bed-wetting, which
had started two years earlier, was reaching alarming propor-
tions. Medications didn't work, because it was not a medical
problem. It was decided that Richard should get treatment at a
nearby centre. There is a discrepancy about who initiated this
treatment plan. The social worker indicates in her reports that
the foster mother and the children had formed strong and
affectionate attachments despite the problems. She indicates,
too, that the foster mother initiated discussions about removing Richard to deal with his bed-wetting. The foster mother,
however, says that the social workers informed her that they
were going to remove him only for a brief period to assess the
psychological components of his bed-wetting and other problems, and that when this was straightened out Richard would
be returned. And Richard?

The day before his move, he was told of the plan to remove
him. He recorded in his diary:

I had 4 hours before I have to leave my family and
friends. I went and got my harmonica. Then I went
down into the woods and I played real slow and sad like
for the occasion. About halfway through the song, my
lower lip began to quiver and I knew I was going to cry
and I was glad so I didn't even try to stop myself. I guess
that [my foster mom] must have heard me and must have
come down to comfort me, but when she put her arm
around me I pulled away and ran up the road aways. I
didn't want no one to love me anymore. I had been hurt
too many times so I began to learn the art of blocking
out the emotions, and I shut the rest of the world out
and the door would open to no one.

The social worker came and took Richard, alone, to his twelfth set of foster parents on a small farm in the nearby town of Westlock, not far from the treatment centre. As the car pulled up to the new home, Richard could see the foster parents at the front entrance down the laneway. He was afraid and bitter. His social worker went out to greet them, leaving Richard alone in the car. When she returned, Richard had locked all the doors, a futile protest against the continuing callous, and to him largely inexplicable, behaviour of those he had come to regard as his jailers. It took two hours to convince him to leave the car. When he finally got out, his social worker took him by the hand and told him to be good and not to worry because "you'll get over it." She left a few minutes later.

His new foster parents, an older couple, directed him to his new quarters. This was the basement with the bare light bulb Richard described in his diary.

Richard Cardinal, Métis, half-breed, a ward of the state that had allegedly "saved" him from his mother's dissolute life, was not yet 10 years old. It was four months before a social worker finally agreed to move him out of these conditions into a home where he would remain for the next four years.

His progress matched, to some degree, the length of his stay. He was well liked by his peers at school, was active in sports and music, for which he had an aptitude, and was "super" with his foster parents' natural children, who tended to look up to him. He was described as always laughing and jumping around.

But there was another side to Richard Cardinal that only infrequently appears in the progress reports or discussions with social workers. His bed-wetting was getting worse, not better. He began to commit delinquent acts such as shooting his foster parents' cow, stealing a car, running away; and his school grades progressively deteriorated. Although these facts came out in discussion with the foster parents, there was a tendency to see Richard as relatively unscathed by his passage through the system and consequently to disregard or remain unconcerned about his adverse behaviours. Ignoring the obvious, you might say.

His diary during this period revealed that he was angry and depressed. "I've got all this anger. I don't know what to do with it." He also noted that he attempted suicide, though there is nothing in the official records to confirm this.

Whatever the actual state of affairs, after four years with these parents with whom he had developed a close if fluctuating relationship, he was told he would have to go because they were going to move to a smaller home and they had no room to keep him. Thus, at 14 years of age Richard was moved to his thirteenth foster home in 10 years. In the next four years he would be moved four more times, be assessed by numerous psychologists, placed in a group home in Edmonton, and attempt suicide on several occasions. His brother Charlie describes one suicide attempt that he was aware of as extremely serious. Richard had been found in an upstairs room, covered in blood and semiconscious. Beside him, scrawled in his blood, was the plea, "Somebody, please help me."

Some time earlier, in 1984, Richard had attempted suicide at school by taking an overdose of drugs. He was rushed to nearby Mayerthorpe Hospital. The attending physician asked for a psychiatric report. The psychologist who examined him determined that he was not suicidal and therefore recommended his discharge. Richard tried again two days later, this time with drugs and alcohol. The ambulance attendants who drove him to the emergency department of Misericordia Hospital in Edmonton from Mayerthorpe, at the suggestion of the attending physician, stated to the doctor there that he had almost died en route. He remained unconscious throughout the night and the following day. By the time he awoke and was able to speak coherently, three physicians had attended him on three successive shifts. The third doctor asked him routinely, "Are you trying to kill yourself?" Richard was said to have responded, "No." The physician, having no other information on hand (no one had documented the earlier attempt), decided that he should be discharged.

Richard phoned his foster parents and asked them to come and pick him up. The foster parents were worried. They felt he was seriously suicidal. They travelled to Edmonton with Charlie and expressed concern to a social worker that Richard was still intent on killing himself. Since they were both employed, they didn't feel they could properly supervise him. The social worker had Richard placed in a youth assessment centre in Grande Prairie, where he remained for nearly two months. In a report to the Department of Social Services and Community Health, it was later observed that "this assessment centre was no more than a holding centre." Very little, if anything, was done in the way of generating psychological profiles with a view to treatment.

Throughout his stay in Grande Prairie, Richard was bitter and angry about being abandoned by his foster parents and "locked up." He had done nothing wrong, to his way of thinking. He refused to abide by any rules until well into his stay and then only because he concluded that it was the only way he would be allowed to leave.

When he was finally released he was informed that he would be going to a new home, since his foster parents still felt that he was suicidal and they could not supervise him closely enough. His new foster parents, the Crothers, were his sixteenth placement, and he was their first. They were told nothing of Richard's behaviour except that he had had a few problems and had been in hospital seeing a psychiatrist. The Crothers say that the social worker spent approximately 20 minutes with them before leaving. The social worker states it was 30 to 40 minutes.

During the subsequent two months Richard worked on his diary, fished with Mr. Crother, and did chores around the farm. He was described as neither friendly nor distant. In June, six months short of his nineteenth birthday, he was found hanging by the barn.

In the aftermath of the boy's death, his family gathered

around him to pay their final respects, something that had not happened during his life. The tragedy also sparked a review of social-work practices in Alberta's Northwest Region, a review that strongly influenced child care policies throughout Alberta. Public outrage and sympathy poured in from across the west in a way that had never been evident during Cardinal's life.

Prof. R. J. Thomlinson, commissioned by the Department of Social Services in Alberta to provide a case-management review, produced a scathing attack on the inadequacies of care that Richard had experienced and that ultimately led to his suicide. He observed in his report that many professionals had expressed concern that "there were hundreds of Richard Cardinals lost in the system." Prompted by Richard's death, critics of child welfare programs began speaking out against a system that routinely mismanages and misshapes the lives of children entrusted to it.

The death of Richard Cardinal had hit a raw nerve in public and professional minds. The press, clamouring as usual for the topical and sensational, headlined the system's failure to provide for Richard, inadvertently undermining the concern that there were hundreds of Cardinals in the system. By focussing solely on one tragedy, the public ignored the system of which Richard was a typical example. Other young people may not be quite as afraid, dependent, or worn out as Richard was, but the betrayals and misunderstandings that followed Richard throughout his short life are similar to those affecting all children in care. Richard Cardinal was not an anomaly within the system; it is just that in death he became more vocal, less private and more public, his heart crying out from the pages of his diary.

In order to see that he is not simply an anomaly but the result of the divergence of social service practice from its policy, we must reconstruct the input of the social workers around him and weigh their actions against their mandate. While reading this analysis, keep in mind that Richard Cardinal had 25 social workers during his adolescent life. If he had had just one or two, one could conclude that they were incompetent and were to blame. But could 25 social workers all be guilty of malpractice? Could all 25 social workers have been operating at a "lower than average" level of skill? Or is it rather that the very system they represent is incapable of properly dealing with such cases?

Professor Thomlinson's report demonstrates that professional practice in this case was grossly inadequate. However, it was not the social workers but their supervisors who were ultimately responsible for the decisions that were made. Policy within child welfare agencies funded by federal governments holds the director of the agency responsible for the agency's decisions. The director relies upon the counsel of his or her supervisors, all of whom will have at least a decade of experience supervising casework, preferably in the relevant geographical area. Richard's case would have passed through the files of at least eight agencies. If the supervisors who oversee the crucial decisions that determine the quality of a child's life in care were all unable to see the impending crisis in Cardinal's life, then the system itself must be judged a failure. It is the supervisors who represent the distilled wisdom of the child welfare decision-making process. Within this complex, supervisors are the link between government regulations and agency policy, and between the ranks of individual social workers and the children who come into care. In this case, it can only be concluded that the entire system failed dismally.

Richard was made a temporary ward of the state when he was originally apprehended, for a period not exceeding 12 months, in keeping with the Alberta Child Welfare Act. By the time he was made a permanent crown ward at 10 years of age, he had been in 12 homes and had 14 workers. The length of stay varied from one week to little more than one year. Some changes of residence were due to the family's medical problems, or to sheer incompetence on the part of foster parents. Other moves were provoked by incompetent social workers who appeared ready to move Richard at the merest hint of a problem rather than work on it in the home. Neither the social workers nor the foster parents were committed to making the ideal of permanency a reality in this boy's life. For Richard, each separation opened the wound of the original separation from his mother, his family, and his Métis heritage. All the homes he passed through were white Anglo-Saxon homes.

The significant personal problems that Richard Cardinal suffered were largely ignored by his social workers or, if noted, were not acted upon in a successful therapeutic manner. While the social workers' progress reports are to be completed, ideally, each month and at least every three months according to Alberta's child welfare policy, this reporting rarely occurred. What notes there were were often inaccurate and scanty. Again, ideally, face-to-face meetings between worker and child should take place, according to the act, at the very least once every three months, and more if the child's condition warrants it. Neither of these rules was followed. When personal visits did occur, they usually signalled another traumatic departure. In this particular case, given the frequency of moves, the escalating behavioural problems, the bed-wetting, and the more frequent bouts of depression, it was patently clear that more vigorous contact was necessary, along with active treatment plans.

When it became obvious that return to the natural parents was not possible, alternative plans with a view towards permanency planning should have been initiated to prevent the child from drifting through the fostering system. In this regard, too, the social workers failed. Furthermore, the foster parents were advised at different times by different social workers to treat Richard's bed-wetting medically, without success. As each social worker changed (there were approximately two a year) new advice was given. There was no continuity because there was no consistent case planning. One social worker encouraged Richard to undergo a psychological assessment; it indicated that Richard was testing the foster parents. This characteristically isolated and uninsightful diagnosis was passed on to untrained foster parents, who then proceeded to act on the advice as if it was true. They would withstand the "testing" by rejecting or ignoring him until he ceased his immature form of behaviour. Treatment at this point turned to punishment, the very opposite of what Richard needed.

In his report, Professor Thomlinson noted that in separate conversations it was repeated to him many times that permanent wards take low priority in the social worker's caseload. Even if true, it does not explain the level of negligence that characterized Richard's entire crown wardship.

Richard desired throughout his life to understand his Métis heritage. Little was ever done about this except to record on two occasions that he was "having problems dealing with his heritage." Few people seem to have been aware of the effect on a Métis child of throwing him into a series of alien, white, rural homes. All the foster parents were untrained, non-Métis, and therefore prone to misunderstand aspects of Richard's behaviour.

The foster parents also expressed frustration over the lack of assistance they were getting from the department's social workers. According to the Alberta child welfare manual, "A social worker is to work in a cooperative partnership with the foster parents with a goal of meeting the total needs of the foster children in the best possible way. . . . They are working *with* the department, not for it."[1] Almost all of Richard's foster parents said that they were inadequately prepared by their workers to deal with a troubled Métis child.

During the final three years in and out of foster and group homes, drinking excessively, more actively aggressive towards others, and suicidal, alternating between rural areas and the city of Edmonton, Richard Cardinal began publicly putting up the final barriers of his resistance. (According to his diary, he had privately begun shutting out the world by the time he was 11 years old.) Sensitive people around him could sense his desperate moods and attempted to get close, but it was too late. Like many Native children before and after him, he had suffered enough.

Is Richard Cardinal a unique case? Is northwestern Alberta like Manitoba or Newfoundland or Ontario? Are all of Canada's social-service supervisors, social workers, and foster parents so indifferent to the fate of their charges? If an inquiry had not been instigated by the actions of John Crother, Richard's death would have gone unnoticed. He would have been just another statistic in an agency's file. Are there many others out there suffering the same fate as Richard?

The evidence, and the testimony of hundreds of young people dependent upon the system, compels me to affirm that Cardinal's case is not unique. The experiences of children in care in Canada, America, and England show us that the system is the same all over. These children share a universe of discredited rights and scarred emotions, which the system caused, exacerbated, and, even at the best of times, failed to heal. "The system" generally is indifferent to the fate of its charges. One can see this clearly just by examining the research on what happens to children when they leave care, and the lack of policies and provisions that would bolster independence. There is no sustained research effort in this area in Canada and limited data in the United States. No one within the child welfare field has deemed it necessary to examine what happens to the children who leave the care of the state at 18 years of age. Where do they go? What do they do? What are their job prospects? How do they manage once they become adults?

Richard Cardinal explained to one foster mother that he was terrified of leaving the care of the state. He felt that he was neither Métis nor white. He had lost his family. He knew nothing more than the series of failed placements that had broken his spirit. He lacked social and employment skills and was grossly undereducated. To go out into the world, to work, to make friends, to do things that other "normal" human beings do was incomprehensible to him, and for this reason terrifying. Had he known how many adolescents in the care of the state, like him, are ill prepared to deal with the outside world from which they were originally rejected, perhaps he would not have felt so alone. Far from being an isolated extreme, Richard Cardinal's life was a testament to all that is wrong within the system.

Nowhere is the breakdown of the bureaucratic child welfare

system, and the dominant middle-class assumptions behind it, more evident than in the treatment of Native people. Since Cardinal's death many Native and Métis children have spoken openly of the abuses they routinely suffered in a system dominated by white child welfare advocates. From their earliest contacts with Euro-Canadians, when they were seen as heathen to be converted, to later traders and settlers who saw them as holding resources to be exploited, Natives in Canada have watched their culture being systematically destroyed. What was once a thriving and diverse culture of hunters and gatherers now faces imminent demise. Excluded from the decision-making process, Natives feel unable to participate in either their own or white culture. They are between two worlds, one that today scarcely exists and one they cannot be part of. The psychological consequences have been devastating: alcoholism, suicide, psychological and physical disorders, and family breakdown are all well above the national average.

Child welfare as it is practised in the northern communities has its roots in, and has advanced, the breakdown of Native culture. Like health and education officials before them, child welfare practitioners have sought to remove children from these pockets of poverty and place them in white foster homes in urban centres far from family, friends, and what little remains of their traditions. Native language and customs were discouraged and ridiculed. Most children were not returned home for long periods, and when they did return they found themselves alienated not only from their family but also from their culture.

The number of Native children in the child welfare system is disproportionately high in northern Ontario, the four western provinces, and the two territories. But despite the traditionally high number of Natives in care, the level of support and preventive intervention is often dismally low. With the exception of what is done in a few bands in Ontario, Manitoba, and British Columbia, Native child welfare services continue to be administered by non-Native social workers. Frequently these white social workers are new to the position, do not speak the language, and do not understand the culture. In order to cover vast territories in an inhospitable environment, they must take shortcuts in the prevention process. Many are simply too overwhelmed by the enormity of the problem. The only solution, it would appear, is to reinvest Native people with autonomy and responsibility both in this specific area and in other areas of their life.

The child welfare system has paid no attention to the ways Native communities have traditionally prevented parental neglect or child care problems: through communal and serial parenting. As with Native medicine and other fundamental social structures, patterns of child care have been so severely interrupted that many Native communities have had great difficulty in re-establishing patterns of community care or in creating local substitute care resources.

The child who is uprooted, however, and placed in a white, lower-middle-class home is implicitly or explicitly "retrained" as a white, lower-middle-class child with the intention of integration or assimilation. If he *should* succeed in forming an identity during this process (difficult even for well-cared-for children) and gain acceptance into the white community, as an adolescent he will very often have to face all over again the question of whom he belongs to, as he rediscovers his Native roots and history.

Virtually no longitudinal studies have looked at the effect that cultural deprivation, or the attempt to straddle two cultures simultaneously, has on Native children in care. It is only during the last two decades that the issue has been explored and not until this decade that autonomous Native bands have taken over the care of their children. But a brief look at the extremely disorganized and destructive cultural patterns indicates that past policies have been universally harmful.

The tragedy in the care of Native children illustrates, among other things, that we should be leery of benevolent programs instituted by governments to solve problems of their own making. It illustrates as well that, rationalizations notwithstanding, social workers complicitly, perhaps naively, abetted tactics reminiscent of cultural paternalism and imperialism under the guise of benevolence.

In the wake of Richard Cardinal's death, the general public joined with outraged Métis and Native groups to challenge the government's role in Native child welfare. The Department of Indian and Northern Affairs undertook a case-by-case review of all permanent crown wards. Critics called for an increase in preventive outreach programs and family support to be pro- vided to Native families in order, wherever possible, to keep Native children within their natural families or with their sib- lings in Native-appointed surrogate families. They sought and obtained specific guidelines and consultative assistance to Native groups wishing to establish autonomous child welfare services. They fought for funding from the federal Depart- ments of Health and Welfare and Indian and Northern Affairs, and from their provincial social services ministries, to initiate a campaign to recruit and train Native foster families. They out- lined the cultural policies that prohibited the balanced and free expression of Native children in relation to their cultural orien- tation. And finally, they encouraged the government to estab- lish an independent Native ombudsman to oversee the implementation of and concurrence with these objectives. As a result, people organizing Native child welfare services have clearer, legislated rights with a mechanism for ensuring that those rights are protected.

Richard Cardinal's death thereby served to bring focus to the problems that were affecting hundreds, indeed thousands of Native children across Canada. The life he led in care that ended in suicide, for others ends in quiet despair, alcoholism, or jail. Natives make up only 2.5 percent of the Canadian population, yet they make up 10 percent of the penitentiary inmates in Canada. In the western provinces, this proportion is even more startling; there, Natives make up 5 percent of the general population and an incredible 32 percent of the prison population. These statistics parallel the proportion of Native youths in care. Only 5 percent of Canada's children are Native, but a full 25 percent of children in care are Native. The figure rises dramatically in western Canada, where fully 60 percent of all crown wards are Native or Métis. According to Philip Hepworth, "a high proportion of Native children who have been in care later appear in correctional facilities."

In a recent report entitled *Locking up Natives in Canada*, sponsored by the federal Department of Justice, the authors noted that the disproportion is growing. They concluded that the justice system is often incomprehensible to Natives and recognizes none of their cultural and spiritual values.

> Placed in historical context, the prison has become for many young people the contemporary equivalent of what the Indian residential school represents for their parents. Although they noted that alcohol is present in many of the offenses, they suggested that it represents an escape typical of a people who have been dispossessed of their land, culturally sublimated and rendered marginal players in society.[2]

Although Cardinal focussed the challenges and highlighted severe problems of Native children in the child welfare system, when all is said and done it would be wrong to pass off his death as only a Native issue. His life and death are, to use the common expression, only the tip of the iceberg. Other youths in care understand and empathize strongly with Cardinal because so many of them have been treated the same way. Ill prepared by their sojourn in the care of the state, reundered powerless through their in-care conditioning, suffering silently, they graduate into the welfare system or eke out a dismal living at menial jobs. It is not a future to look forward to, and many of them, like Cardinal, attempt suicide. The routine mishandling of Cardinal's case due to overload, displaced priorities, bad supervision, and basic ignorance of the "marginal players" is endemic in the child protection system. Each time an inquiry probes for abuses within the system, many children come forward with the same message. It is heart-rending to hear it repeated that youth in care are afraid or feel it useless to speak out unless compelled by the circum-

stances of a public inquiry, at which time their private night-
mares become public spectacles.

Consider the words, for instance, of Shane Earle, a key
witness at the inquiry into the Mount Cashel orphanage, in St.
John's, Newfoundland. He said that he and many other young
boys were repeatedly sexually and physically abused by Brothers at the orphanage, but he could get no one within the church
or the social services to act on his complaints. He attempted
suicide shortly after a 1975 criminal investigation into the
accusations against the Brothers at the orphanage was
abruptly terminated, without explanation. He did it, he said,
"because they were not going to do anything. They just left us
there. Like that . . . in those conditions. When it happened like
it did and there were a lot of us and we couldn't do anything, it
felt like they shut the door on us and society really didn't care
about what happened to the kids at Mount Cashel."

His fears were echoed by Derek O'Brien, who as a young
abandoned boy was put into a foster home where he was forced
to live in a cold, dark basement, beg like a dog for his food at
which time he would be called Fido, walk several blocks to go
to the bathroom at a local dump because his foster mother
wouldn't let him use the one in the house, and endure more
equally horrendous treatment. He had kept his secret for 15
years because he, like Shane Earle, with whom he later resided
at Mount Cashel, feared that no one would believe him and
that nobody cared. They felt, truly, like nobody's children.

How many others have remained silent? How much has the
system improved since then? What were the issues here? Power
and powerlessness. A sense of futility. The feeling that nobody
cared. These are still the issues. And if these sensational or
large-scale abuses can remain quiet for so long, how much
easier for isolated but equally damaging cases to go unre-
dressed? How will society respond to the systematic, less spec-
tacular, but widespread abuses? How do we prove that we
care?

We must move now, as many radical social-service providers
have been urging, to a more complete preventive model. We

must redesign the current system from top to bottom. Otherwise hundreds of Richard Cardinals, white and Native, immigrant and poor, will continue to be pushed aside and forgotten.

7

LET THE CHILDREN SPEAK

*John Meston sat in the foyer of the McMan Youth Centre
in Edmonton's east end. "Another one," he was thinking
to himself. "We had him, and then poof, he's gone, just
like that." He was thinking about Murray: a black homo-
sexual teenager, dead by suicide. How many had to die to
make a point? How many had to die before the system
changed?*

*Meston, the recently appointed director of McMan
Youth Centre, was well known among the social-work
crowd in Edmonton. There were varying opinions. He
he'd worked miracles with some kids, but he was unpredictable. You never knew what he was going to do next.
Bureaucrats were wary. But on the whole, it was felt that
what he did worked, and wasn't that what the system was
all about?*

*Meston had been hit hard by the recent death of Richard
Cardinal. He knew the track record for dealing with Native
youth was appalling. The youths he had spoken with were
equally affected, but more sanguine. "That's the way it is.
You just gotta be tougher," they intoned together, pictures
of studied indifference, which he knew masked their impo-
tence to change the way the system constricted their lives.
And these were the bright ones, the sensitive ones, who had
responded and for some reason — usually they had found a*

135

mentor — had gotten up off the roller-coaster of their life in care and begun to shake themselves and the system. They could be reached; but the others, the hundreds, maybe thousands, of Cardinals out there who couldn't or wouldn't get up, who had been beaten into submission to archaic and insensitive principles, what could be done to reach them before it was too late?

Meston had been working to inspire a group of child care workers, young and ideal, not yet hardened by the system of which he was now an administrative instrument. He himself had been trained in the child care worker tradition. These rank-and-file members spend more time per day per child than any other member of the helping profession. It was the child care worker, educated in two-year community college programs, or university graduates who stumbled into the profession, who patrolled the halls of residential houses, group homes, and the few progressive community programs that catered to youths. They were younger than social workers, more recently trained, and not much older than some of the kids who passed through McMan Youth Centre. They were enthusiastic, at least initially. And Meston, now in a position of power, wanted to channel their idealism and utilize their time to the maximum advantage of the kids.

It was a radical idea. Child care workers got paid one-third to one-half as much as their counterparts in social work. They were at the low end of the totem pole in their profession. There was limited career-advancement opportunity and limited input into the decisions that affected a youth's life in care. As a result, most child care workers became frustrated and burnt out quickly. Meston wanted to harness their untainted idealism before the system drummed it out of them.

He would hold informal weekly sessions in which everyone, staff and kids, would participate. For the first time in their lives for many of the kids, an adult with

*authority over them was letting them speak, and was
actually listening. Meston would philosophize about
aspects of change. You can't fight the system from outside, he would say with conviction. If you want to be an
agent of change you have to fight from within. You have
to bend your ideals to fit in with prevailing attitudes and
when you see the chance, you then try to shape the attitude. Change, though slow, would follow.*

*Meston had taken his own philosophy to heart. As an
administrator, he had removed himself from the ranks of
child protection to establish a different type of bureaucracy. His board of directors were willing to accept some
changes from this compassionate, maverick thinker, but
not quite everything he proposed. They wanted to maintain a neat, efficient, bureaucratic structure. Top heavy.
Committees. No individual decision making, but always
referring up to someone else. Meston was at the pinnacle
of everything he least desired. But change slowly was
working its way through the system. Too slowly, he was
thinking as he slumped down in his seat and wondered
about Murray and the others they missed. How many
would it take to make a point?*

Throughout the centuries, dependent children have been victims of a system designed to corral them into various saving programs. They have been labelled, branded, trained, almost as if they were horses or dogs being taught to obey the commands of superiors, without ever having a say in the proc-ess that shaped their lives. It is interesting that many of the adults I spoke with who had been in foster care or institutions when they were younger had forgotten the details of their early lives. There are no milestones, no highlights. It is as if they had no history to speak of, or that the events they did remember were meaningless and did not cohere into a logical pattern; perhaps they unconsciously felt the need to obliterate the past, to drive it back into the depths of the psyche and get on with their lives.

During interviews it was disconcerting to watch as a number of seemingly well adjusted adults broke down as they began recalling buried memories of abuse they had suffered at the hands of foster parents and institutional staff. One young man said:

> I'm 30 now and I want to get on with my life, so I try not to think much about it, but when something calls it up and I do have to think about it, it's like I'm six years old again, a little boy, and I'm in the room and my foster mom is there and she's hit me and I'm in a corner, a little boy with no shoes, and I'm crying and I can't look at her and she's saying, "Look at me when I'm talking to you," and I'm crying and I can't look up and I can't see her through the tears and all I want is for someone to come and hug me and hold me and make it all go away. It's very real, like I'm right there. There are many different scenes like this. At night, I clench my teeth so bad they are all ground down, and I sweat and wake up crying out, and my wife's saying, "It's okay, Danny, it's just a dream." I guess that's how I get it out, instead of letting it get to me during the day. If it weren't for that, maybe I'd be a mess now.[1]

Another reason for the absence of a remembered past is that children in care had no say in their lives. All choices were made for them. They acquired a habitual attitude of dependence, which ceded the need for thought or choice to others. Not ever having had to take responsibility or think for themselves, they have few personally significant experiences to recall. The history we hear of these children is history told by the adults who controlled them.

Although that attitude and the assumptions that generated it still pervade the system, substantial change is occurring. Adolescents in care are beginning to find their own voice, to speak up and feel their potency to effect change. And if anything can produce dramatic change in a structure as inert as the child care bureaucracy, it is this group of empowered youth, whose hopeful vision and exuberant self-interest will cut through the myopia of the adults around them.

The story begins indirectly, in England, from where a unique idea spread into Canada, starting in the west before heading to Ottawa under the auspices of the Canadian Child Welfare Association. It is carried along by young people, aged 14 to 24, who are struggling, scared, enthusiastic. In less than three years an idea shared by only a handful of youths has grown into a positive reality influencing the lives of thousands of youths across Canada. They call themselves the Canadian National Youth in Care Network.

In England in the late 1970s, a group of youths in state care sparked the development of an organization that would be run by youths in, or recently in, foster and institutional homes. At their original conference, sponsored by Britain's National Children's Bureau, more than a hundred youths between the ages of 14 and 18 participated in discussions related to their perceptions of "being cared for." At the end of that conference, it was suggested that they start a network among youth in care to further develop and maintain a collective voice to speak on all issues relevant to their lives. In its initial stages this somewhat raucous contingent tended to worry adults within the child welfare system with their highly critical comments and their dissatisfaction with the status quo. They made people feel uncomfortable, and possibly, if the truth were known, a little guilty.

In 1979, independent of the Children's Bureau and other adult parties, a group of adolescents formed the National Association of Young People in Care (NAYPIC) to further their aims. In the process they alienated even more adults, but by this time they had gained a sense of identity outside the systems and people upon whom they had originally been dependent. Christine Lerner, one of the founding members of NAYPIC, states:

We had arrived at the point where we could see that

what we were doing was not only important for us, for youth in care, but for everyone who was involved, or pretended to be involved in the care of children. We realized — and this was new for many of us — that we could be independent, and that we could educate by example. I suppose you could say we were converted, and you know how hard it is to dissuade someone who is converted.[2]

Most of the youths in the association had been labelled slow learners, unskilled, or troublesome. Most had minimal education and had never been involved in any such project. Many had been classified as hard-core delinquents. But they had spirit and a fairly clear idea of what they needed, and as the years went by and their vision expanded they gained a widening sense of immense possibility.

The problems they encountered were indicative of misguided adult perceptions about the needs of children in care. Initially, despite NAYPIC's demonstrated commitment to needy youth, despite their growing list of references and their unassailable accomplishments in helping troubled youth regain their equilibrium, they were unable to obtain charitable status, which cut them off from many sources of funding. Nevertheless, in spite of the lack of resources, the lack of training, and the indifference or outright hostility of the child welfare system, they produced numerous books and pamphlets discussing relevant child welfare issues, organized national conferences, and developed able spokespersons from a number of local groups developing across Britain. They were also recognized by the British media as a significant voice for issues in child welfare. Although NAYPIC still has much to learn about organization, and perhaps about human nature and reconciliation too, they have at last begun to overturn the paternalism that has for centuries characterized the relationship between child savers and children.

NAYPIC's mandate is to promote the views and opinions of young people in care, support and develop local groups, and educate themselves and the public on all aspects of the needs and views of young people in care. They have had an undeniable influence on the British child welfare system.

For example, a survey was sent out to state wards in Britain, most of them in the age range of 13 to 17. The survey was concerned with social service reviews, a process whereby adults involved in the child's life comment on and make decisions about the child's future without any input from the child. The association wished to take issue with the attitude that the child could not possibly comment intelligently on his or her own future, an attitude leading to the feeling of powerlessness shared by so many children in care. Many of the youths responding to the questionnaire had no idea what was at stake; they just responded to the question "What do you think about Reviews?" as they would to one of their peers. The following answers were representative of their responses:

> The social workers and teachers first go in and discuss you and then you are brought in and told of the decision that they have made.
> Well there is people. . . . they are all sitting there and you go in, sit down. They start talking to you about yourself. And then you do what they say.

The overwhelming feeling of most respondents was that they were like mannikins, pulled and pushed by the adults around them, without any effort to take into consideration their own thoughts, feelings, or hopes. This total dependence gradually eroded their desire to even bother to make plans or to act as though they could influence their own future in any way. For their part, adults regarded this passive acceptance of their decision-making role as the way it was and the way it had to be.

NAYPIC's role in this and related issues was to reveal the level of dependence to both the youths and the social workers, then make both parties see that this was not in the best interests of either the children or the wider society and that it could be changed. This required educating adolescents in care about their rights and responsibilities, either by persuading them that they could make choices or by jarring and challenging their semi-institutionalized, dependent attitude. Adults too had to be shown that only if adolescents were given the freedom to make their own decisions, in small issues at first but in increasing importance, could they eventually become well-adjusted members of society.

In a fascinating reversal, it was the children who were educating the adults. One of the important side effects of this growing self-confidence was that when youth in care felt personally empowered and had gained a stronger sense of selfhood, they were in a position to stop the physical and emotional abuses endemic to the system. The issue of powerlessness, though, is only one of myriad issues that NAYPIC has struggled to identify and eradicate.

In a larger context, NAYPIC is a brotherhood, a coalition of like-minded individuals. The constant moving, the feelings of not belonging and of alienation, are overcome by the sense of empowerment experienced by those working together for change. The constructive changes they are able to effect in the system they depend on, and the capacity of youths in care to care for other youths, empathetically, in a way that few adults could, is in itself an emancipating force. As one youth put it:

> Today, I seem just fine to you, don't I? I speak clearly, I laugh a lot, I'm working hard and productively, and I like the people I work with and the kind of work we do, and when you pull that all together you get a fairly happy guy.
>
> But six years ago, when I first got involved, I was like a little puppy dog. You could drag me around by the collar and I'd just follow along. I wasn't happy, but I wasn't that unhappy either, just — I don't know how to say it — just there, doing whatever it was that was required of me.
>
> But gradually, as I began to work with some of the people in NAYPIC, and I was forced to problem-solve along with everyone else — we do a lot of that here —

and come up with solutions that would help me and other kids in my position [in care], I began to feel that I could change things, really make a difference. And I began to resent my little puppy dog act and I had to work on that, and I did. I still am. But today I'm a totally different individual than I was then. Now, when I see a kid like me who's 15 or so and he's feeling a little lost, I can understand just where he is and just how far he's got to go, and I let him know that. Now I'm always on the lookout for solutions, and when you're in that frame of mind guess what happens? You start finding them.[3]

It is the feeling of self-worth and the possibility of finally belonging that I believe will in the long run become the most significant factor in altering the direction of an institution that has controlled their lives in such a suffocating way and continued the abuse that many of them suffered even before they entered the system. And not just in England. As more and more youths in other countries became aware of and inspired by the results of the British organization, they realized that they shared a universe of discredited rights. The assumptions that guided British child savers, it turns out, were the same assumptions that guided child savers in Australia and North America.

In Canada, as early as 1973 there were sporadic attempts to involve youths in the decisions affecting their lives. The Catholic Children's Aid Society of Toronto obtained a grant to develop a newsletter by and about youth in care. Social workers encouraged young people to speak up about whatever troubled them, in the belief that by openly sharing their own experiences the youths would come to see that they were common experiences. The idea was good, though the political climate at the time was not yet concerned with fundamental rights and freedoms of children. It is only recently that this concern, manifesting itself at all levels of society, has opened the door to such openness. So the commitment then on the part of adults and youths was short-lived.

During the late 1970s, progressive social workers at the Ottawa-Carleton Children's Aid Society initiated what they called an independence camp for young people, providing them with a structure to discuss issues of concern to them. This idea was adopted by a number of Societies in Ontario and is still being used with success. It provides an outlet for frustrations, a forum for the exchange of ideas, and a program that teaches youth the skills necessary to deal with independence, a spectre that looms large in the mind of every dependent youth I have spoken with.

McMan Youth Centre in Edmonton proved to be another hotbed of ideas for empowering youth. McMan was staffed primarily with child care workers committed to the idea, planted by John Meston, that youth know best about what affects their lives. Meston — under whose auspices the Canadian equivalent to Britain's NAYPIC would eventually unfold — directed the staff to listen to youths and not impose their ideas without getting the youths' input. By 1983 Meston operated a semi-democratic decision-making process with all ideas passed, as usual, before the board of directors, but then down to the staff and the youths for input. The final decisions, while still in the hands of supervisor Meston and ultimately the board of directors, were therefore sensitive to the input from the bottom end of the bureaucratic structure. Meston suggests an analogy to understand his way of operating. He turns an organizational chart upside down, thus putting the client — the youths — at the top and the board of directors at the bottom. "Our mandate," he says, "is to serve the youths who come to us. Generally they get lost in the bureaucratic shuffle. And unfortunately, what's good for us is not always, maybe not often, good for them."

However, the model that Meston proposed is difficult, if not impossible, to maintain within the current system. It lacks bureaucratic accountability and efficiency. It requires an endless supply of long-term, extremely dedicated workers sharing a vision. To sustain the two — a flexible bureaucracy and a visionary work force — is extremely difficult. It didn't quite live up to Meston's expectations, and the unnecessary obstacles he had to contend with wore him down.

Although Meston's ideal continues to function as a fine example, the style of management he envisioned and implemented was short-lived. But during his tenure it was effective in challenging and assisting youths to speak out. Many of those who would later work towards the development of other progressive models were empowered by McMan and were optimistic enough to see the potential for a strong voice for children in care. Meston planted the idea of a network among a number of youths he worked with, many of whom would later acknowledge him as a friend, mentor, and founding member of the Canadian Youth in Care Network.

In 1979, the same year a group of teenagers in England was forming NAYPIC, Dr. Kathleen Kudfeldt, of the Alberta Association of Social Workers, organized a conference involving 100 young people, relevant professional organizations, and government representatives. She set up the conference in such a way that the youths and the adults would both contribute to the discussion — a provocative idea for that time. The gathering (named, aptly, the Who Cares? Conference) was emotionally heated, as one after the other the children criticized the presentations by the professional social workers. "What do you really know about our needs?" one asked. Another yelled out, "What we were saying and what you are hearing gotta be two different animals." At one point, the youths refused to participate in the discussions, preferring instead to brainstorm and share among themselves what it meant to be in care. For many, it was the first time they had had the opportunity to speak honestly and openly to each other about their confused feelings. They discovered that they understood each other.

Whereas the youths were emotionally charged and challenged by the experience, the sponsoring organizations and attending professionals were made uneasy by the emotional outbursts of the children and went away with negative feelings about the conference. The adolescent emotionalism they had witnessed seemed too naive, hostile, and unpredictable to be effective in dealing with issues related to care. Since the youths were refusing to operate under the adults' control, they were seen to be *out* of control. So although the idea of a nation-wide movement was gaining ground, the project was aborted before it could effectively get started because youths could not secure the establishment's support and could not conceive of a way to get started without it.

Conferences took place sporadically over the next few years, but it was not until five years after the Who Cares Conference that the youths' shared insights and experiences were rekindled.

In 1985, a number of youths and adults who continued to believe in the possibility of institutionalized youths taking responsibility for their own lives formed the Alberta Association for Youth in Care. Again, the impetus came largely through the efforts of John Meston. There were no funds immediately available and no one with credible experience to campaign for a large national youth network. Instead, relying on summer employment programs and supported by their common vision, three young adults began exploring the possibilities. What pushed the association into place finally was the work of a 22-year-old former street kid, now a legend among youths in the Network, Dallas Nicholai.[4]

Dallas knew well what it meant to be in care. He had been a ward from age 11 to 18 and had been in almost every type of facility and program. He says that he started stealing mail from boxes along his paper route and cashing the cheques he found, waiting impatiently to be caught — this was his plan for getting away from his stepfather, who beat him almost daily. It worked. But he wasn't sure the system was that much better than home: "I wasn't prepared for the system, being locked up, having decisions made about my treatment without consulting me, being unable to complain about being beaten by staff for fear of what would be done to me. I felt completely helpless."[5]

Shortly after leaving care at 18, with limited education and even less skill, like many youths before and after him he turned to the streets. He went on welfare, hustled, committed petty crimes, and — just survived. He fell in with other marginal adolescents and would have remained there had it not been for a fortuitous series of meetings with an adult worker who pushed and prodded and gently guided him away from the street. He became involved with a group, most of whose participants came from the McMan Youth Centre, who like him were working through their turbulent adolescence with a minimum of adult guidance. They spoke of taking control of their lives, of responsibility, of wrongs within the system that they could redress. They spoke heatedly of being thrown out onto the street at 18 with no prospects. No wonder they turned to crime or prostitution, they said to each other. No wonder they felt so hurt, so abandoned.

In the background, Meston broadened their insight with information on rights and freedoms and with news about others like them who were seeking to change the system. They began to think of themselves romantically as freedom fighters. Dallas became obsessed with the possibility of a nation-wide network of youth in care. He began to do some research. He gathered support for the idea from within the child welfare system. When the group learned of the British network, they quickly organized a visit to England to gain first-hand experience and knowledge of that association. They succeeded in persuading various provincial and federal ministries and agencies to sponsor them.

The delegation to England learned from their British counterparts about the obstacles they would face. They heard about NAYPIC's mistakes, about how they would do it differently if they could do it over again. The Canadian contingent saw with their own eyes that the vision of empowered youth had become a reality. Their British elder brothers and sisters were proof. All that remained was to bring the struggle home.

Whereas the earlier, less ambitious attempts at forming a national coalition had quickly petered out, now the momentum was supported by adults *within* the system who foresaw the impending crisis in foster care. As well, the political climate was radically changing in the wake of the evolving Canadian Charter of Rights and Freedoms. Legislation that sought to entrench the rights of the child in all provincial child welfare constitutions enabled youths to speak with authority about the letter of the law as it affected their lives. Dallas, Troy Rypstra, and others travelled across the country meeting with interested and supportive adults, attempting to convey their vision to youth in care.

Dallas Nicholai is representative of the kind of youths who, given the opportunity, demonstrate remarkable abilities. Adults within the system appreciated his directness, even when his ideas, seemingly impractical and unsophisticated, but somehow true nonetheless, conflicted with their own. Other youths in care understood him perfectly. He was speaking their language, proclaiming their common experience in a message he carried from one side of the country to the other.

> Do you want to leave care and live on the street? Are you afraid of leaving care? Have you ever thought to yourself the only way out is suicide or enough drugs to keep the pain away? Do you think there's a way out?
>
> Well there may be a way out, but you have to find it. You have to take control of your life. I don't have all the answers, but we have strength in our numbers, and the more among us who know what rights are ours, what possibilities are open to us, the more we have the chance to be free. We don't have to live in fear. We don't have to depend on the system. We don't have to be subservient. Knowledge is power. We can change things.[6]

The vision Dallas espoused struck some as a revelation. To a growing number of disenchanted youths across the country, Dallas Nicholai became a champion who in turn had found a "champion" in the power of the group, the key to breaking out of isolation, through mutual *inter*dependence.

At a Vancouver conference in 1986 attended by a motley crew of youths from across Canada, some who had been working separately and others who had heard rumours of the development, there was clear consensus that the time had come to unite efforts. For the adults and the youths in attendance, it was a profoundly moving conference, and it launched this Canadian association of youth in care officially onto the national child welfare stage.

That year, they gained formal status, naming themselves the Canadian National Youth in Care Network. Since then they have made a significant impression on a wide spectrum of officials involved in the child welfare industry. They have lobbied governments, started regional and national newsletters, and published position statements on independence training, youth on the street, and adolescent prostitution. They are currently being called upon when government commissions seek input on issues relating to youth care. They prepare presentations, outlining their views at major social-work conferences. They have solicited and obtained support from many child welfare professionals, and they have made it a matter of policy to seek out professional opinion while not necessarily or always deferring to that opinion. This is, of course, a contentious area, one that handcuffed the British network.

The British youths saw their task as one of trying to free themselves from the centuries of indifference and paternalism that characterized their relationship to child welfare authorities. They realized, though, that they were also in very real ways dependent on those adults for the support of their embryonic organization. The concept of empowerment rests on the idea that youth in care can and should become responsible for the quality of their lives, yet their success still depended to a large degree on adults who, with their greater experience and maturity, were capable of helping the adolescents achieve their goals. If knowledge was power, it was the system that was most powerful because it had the most knowledge. In time they gathered amongst themselves those who had the necessary knowledge, and reliance on adults thereby diminished, but initially this continued dependence was an uncomfortable circumstance. It was felt by some that to "go to bed with our oppressors" would compromise them. The goal, after all, was to wrest control from the adults. It was also argued that not *everyone* had a bad experience in care. Not all adults in the system were indifferent, incompetent, or insensitive. Indeed, most of the youths in care who had early on become active in the network had done so through the assistance of an adult who believed in the youths and the organization's goals. In the long run, the British association decided, it was the cooperative efforts of adults and youth that would further their goal of transforming a system of control into a system of care that would guarantee certain inalienable rights to youths both entering and coming out of the system. But the struggle between the two factions — those who welcomed adult help and those who didn't — hampered the association for a long time.

Learning from their British counterparts, the Canadian Network worked on this issue from the start. They decreed that only youths between the ages of 14 and 24 could remain active voting members within the organization. This, they felt, would ensure that all members were in touch with the changing issues of youth in care and set a limit to the adult preoccupations that might tend to compromise their goals. Adults were relegated to non-voting status and would serve as board members. It was a wise decision that has taken them a long way in their struggle towards emancipation. By soliciting adult opinion and knowledge, they have fostered a spirit of cooperation with almost all levels within the social services, at the same time preserving their integrity. Many professionals have welcomed the organization as an idea whose time has come. The difficulty will be in maintaining their orientation and enthusiasm without being co-opted by the very system they seek to change.

Some of the adult scepticism and animosity that attended earlier attempts to organize remains. Some workers feel threatened by the fact that their youthful clients are usurping their control. The youths whom they had believed incapable of anything more than servile occupations, and whom they merely herded on their way to welfare rolls, were now acting in ways that didn't fit with those assumptions. The child workers were being told that much of what they had been doing was ineffective and damaging — by the very people on whose behalf they believed they were working. But only the most insensitive caseworker could fail to hear the ring of truth in what these youths were saying, even if some of them were saying it inarticulately and free of child savers' jargon.

If, as I have stated, these youths have significantly influenced the way adults now deal with youth in care, with the potential for still more far-reaching consequences, they have also changed the way they deal with each other. In the process of delivering themselves by their own hand from the paternalism of their caretakers, they are embarking on a liberating journey of discovery. They find relief in having found a family, someone who understands them and a group they can belong to. If it is true (as will be explored in detail in the last chapter) that youth in care often find themselves on the street or in other undesirable situations searching for the family they never had and further alienating themselves from the mainstream society that rejected them, then this formation of a different, new kind of "extended family" must be seen as a profoundly important development. Membership becomes a ticket to meaning, friendship, and a horizon of possibilities. Adolescents for whom the Network works become further models of the possibilities open to all youth, and the power of the fraternity is thus compounded and grows even more rapidly.

The feeling of being misunderstood, and consequently feeling out of place wherever she went, was eloquently stated by a youth from the Network who was taken into care when she was 11 years old.

> I was always told that I was the problem. Wherever I went, I figured that if something went wrong it was me who was to blame. I'd say to workers that my dad was terrible. He wouldn't hit me physically, but he used to shit on me anytime I said or did anything. I mean anything. My brothers and sisters were okay. It was just me. I'd get into trouble of some kind, I was always in some

kind of trouble and the police would come around, or
the school would phone up. And the workers would look
around and they'd take my father's word that I was the
problem. Eventually I began to agree with everyone.

Now, though, when I look back at my family I can see
that I was being used, for reasons I can't yet figure out,
as a scapegoat. As long as they had me to blame, they
were okay. But what do you think it did to me? . . . The
worst time was when they'd take me back home for a
trial visit to see if they could get us back together. It
never worked 'cause my family didn't want me and each
time I thought, "Shit, I must be awful," and every time I
went back to my foster parents I set out to prove, or at
least that's how I explain it, just how bad I was.

And then they'd turf me out and I'd end up somewhere else, like it just went on. I ended up in seven
homes in three years. I got sadder and sadder and the
sad part of it was, nobody knew I was sad. They thought
I was just bad. And until recently, until I met the guys in
the Network, that's exactly what I thought. I haven't
quite got it figured out yet, but at least now I feel like
there are other people around like me. We got problems,
sure, but hell, we can work them out.[7]

This young woman is now an integral part of the movement.
As she shared her experience with others in a local group she
had joined she discovered that there were a lot of other adolescents out there who on the surface are "creepy little kids who
have come to believe that they are useless, and who wants to
deal with creepy, useless kids?" Recognizing herself in these
others and sharing her experience with them helped her, and
them, to come to terms with their experiences and to reject the
labels that had dogged them through the system. It isn't over
for her — the feelings of loss, the struggle to reconcile the good
and the bad of the past and the uncertainty of the present —
but someone along the way recognized the sad little girl in her

trying to find a way out of her predicament, and now, among her peers in the Network, she feels stronger, more hopeful. The Network had proved to be her salvation.

The commonality of experience that Canadian and British youths discovered has been reaffirmed in the United States, where the Canadian group is being used as a model for local groups emerging in Chicago, Washington, D.C., and cities in Nebraska, California, Minnesota, New York, and Ohio. All across North America, the parameters of their experience have been the same: low expectations, channelling into vocational or easily managed behavioural programs, severe emotional damage, the fear of independence, and the lack of resources to deal with their common needs, and a metaphorical gag that appeared whenever they tried to speak about these realities. They began to understand that their problems were not simply repercussions of their pre-care life or their idiosyncratic personal flaws, but a direct result of their experience in the care of the state. In many cases the youth organizations' research revealed flagrant abuses by foster parents or child welfare organizations.

One such story became a rallying cry for the children in care in Britain. It was the life story of Gaskin, a long-term violent criminal who coauthored a book about his childhood in care. He speaks with horror of his early years in the home of his foster mother, a Mrs. Johnson:

> She was annoyed at having a child in the house all day, and my time was spent on out-of-the-way chairs, keeping quiet. When I was naughty she stripped me and stood me in the bath, then threw buckets of cold water over me. She knew her stuff, that lady. Later the same trick was to be used on me by the screws in Wormwood Scrubs, though by that time they had to put me in a straight jacket and a padded cell to get away with it. When she took me out of the bath Mrs. Johnson rubbed me briskly with a towel like sandpaper, then made me

stand naked on the landing. "Go on, stand there. Face
the wall. Little devil" ... for hours on end.[8]

The response to the publication that detailed similar abuses
was overwhelming. The public was outraged. Hundreds of
former wards of the state (many of them now prisoners) wrote
to say that they had suffered similar treatment while in the care
of the state and demanded an immediate review of a system
that could do such things to abandoned children. In America
and Canada, beatings by foster parents are not uncommon,
especially in rural areas, as recent inquiries such as the one on
Newfoundland's Mount Cashel home operated by the Christian Brothers have shown. But youth networks tend to shy
away from this sensational aspect of life in care. They state that
it is unclear how many abusive foster parents there are and that
such cases only capture public imagination for a moment,
deflecting attention away from the underlying issues of powerlessness, rootlessness, and the profound sense of alienation
that many youths in care suffer. Only by first responding to and
changing the fundamental belief system of youth in care and
by reassigning power over the lives of children in care can the
resultant problems of physical or sexual abuse by foster parents be addressed.

This overwhelming consensus of the children in care contra-
dicts the idea that the state is there to nurture its wards or to
provide them with the advantages they presumably were
deprived of in their natural families. In the United States,
where research has been undertaken for a much longer time
and the foster system has come under close scrutiny, the Child
Welfare League of America (which is sponsoring the development of an American youth-in-care network) has labelled the
foster system "a national disgrace." Wide-ranging recommendations for change are being actively solicited, and youths in
care intend to play a crucial role in the changes that take place.
It will require an enormous amount of self-sacrifice and stub-
born determination on the part of youths to rearrange the

perspectives of traditionalists within the child welfare system, but no one else is going to do it for them.

John Meston observed that the level of organization the Canadian youths were capable of surprised everyone:

> Adults in the system hearing about their endeavours were supportive, but they were really floored by the level of skill these guys demonstrated once they got started. The adults are used to the obstacles and the egos of other adults getting in the way of proposed changes. They see the practical need for funds and the need for committees to get the go-ahead for their projects, all of which takes time and none of which is predictable in terms of outcome. That's just the way it is.
>
> But these kids had enthusiasm and were sustained by the growing sense that what they did mattered not only to them but to youth all over. Given a cause, given a sense of responsibility and a choice in their lives, given the opportunity to do something that *meant* something to them, these youths have broken every mould that we in the services have shaped for them. It impresses and slightly unnerves people. Even when they see it, they still find it hard to believe what these youths are doing.[9]

Previously, accepting the diminished expectations of the adults around them, these young people did not imagine they could perform complex organizational tasks, write and give speeches, learn what they needed to stay on top of things, keep up with tight schedules, and perform myriad, often tedious tasks necessary to a formal organization.

Somehow the statistics penned by professional students of the system, which document similar trends or inadequacies about the quality of care, seem far more riveting when commented on by those who directly suffer the consequences of those inadequacies. The Network serves as an information clearing house and a self-help outlet, and is also capable of rigorous assessments of the system. Thus it serves a double role as a trouble-shooter and a self-regulating eliminator of the flaws it identifies. This aspect of the Network is crucially important to understand, both for youths in the Network and for those willing to work with them. As these youths begin to trade their stories, their commonality illustrates that the level of insensitivity among social workers and child welfare authorities, and their ability to misunderstand completely what a youth experiences, is the norm rather than the exception.

In his recently published book, *To Be on Our Own with No Direction from Home*, Brian Raychaba articulates the views of youth in care. Formerly a youth in care himself, he is currently completing his university education. His comments bear close scrutiny. They are the clearest statements to date on the history of child welfare in Canada, and they present the unadulterated views of the youths inside the child protection programs. Though Raychaba often speaks in the language of the adult researchers whose comments he examines at length, he relates those findings to the actual experience, the raw, gut-wrenching reality that youth in care confront daily.

He writes in his preface:

> During my seven-and-a-half year "tour" of the care sys-
> tem,. . . I had the privilege of living with and encounter-
> ing individuals whose life experiences and circumstances
> differed greatly from my own. These were fellow pro-
> gram residents — young people in care, some of whom,
> even though two to three years older than me, were far
> less developed and mature both emotionally and
> socially, who, even as they approached the age of major-
> ity, were still struggling to complete grade nine or ten at
> a basic level of instruction, and who had either never
> worked or who possessed none of the "know how"
> needed to find, get and keep a job. . . . While in care, I
> came to the startling conclusion that in many respects, I
> was the exception — a child welfare anomaly. Imagine
> my surprise upon discovering that I was one of the only

two young people in the care of my agency (a large
urban Catholic Children's Aid Society in Ontario) to go
on to university.[10]

He notes too the increasing number of young people coming
into care who are severely abused sexually, physically, and
emotionally. Many youths, damaged by their pre-care experience, expressed their fear of other, more violent youths in the
system with whom they often came in contact. The child welfare system is incapable of distinguishing and giving appropriately different care to children who are almost "normal" and
those who are violent or severely traumatized. Indeed, the
levels of drug and alcohol abuse among youth in care, coupled
with their increasingly aggressive behaviour, leads one to think
that the care experience is becoming increasingly dangerous
for those who reluctantly enter it.

Raychaba cites a 1986 study entitled *Rights of Passage: A
Study of the Mental Health Needs of Transitional Age Youth in
Metro Toronto*, which put the matter succinctly:

> The agencies [three Toronto Children's Aid Societies]
> underlined that the most disturbed youth, who have
> diagnosed psychiatric disorders, autism, or high-risk
> behavioral difficulties, all tend to be in the older age
> group. It was added that most of these youth were in the
> child welfare system at an earlier age, but they were not
> diagnosed until later, or became worse over time.[11]

Many of the younger youths report being placed in overcrowded residential homes with these older adolescents. This,
of course, is a crucial aspect of the foster care crisis. With the
shortage of foster homes, many apprehended children completely bypass this first, theoretically benign stage of state-
sponsored care and go straight into group homes, where they
encounter situations as troublesome, or more so, than their
family situation.

As with Richard Cardinal, the transiency of their life is one
of the most frequent complaints of children in care. They feel

ghettoized, like gypsies moving from one place to another, without any rationale for the frequency of their enforced movement. At a 1986 conference in Hamilton, Ontario, Jane McSherry — one of 60 youths in care invited to attend — explained to social workers in the audience that youths from across Canada had complained vigorously about being moved time and time again. She cited the statistics. She confirmed the despondency it had engendered in her and her peers. Another young person described life in care as something akin to a "pinball", bouncing crazily around in every direction. Jane then spoke of an inability to form relationships, the difficulties of trusting adults, and the need for stability.

These youths cannot be discounted, nor held at bay by statistics or case studies cited in textbook after textbook speaking abstractly about the effects of separation and loss. These youths, speaking out at conferences across the country, are the flesh-and-blood results of years in the system. Each time they speak out, they are reconstructing the perspective from which social workers will think of them in the future. As one social worker, jarred by her encounter with youths from the Network, put it,

> When you've talked till you're blue in the face with a kid who has tried to commit suicide a dozen times, when you've reached out to her, given her what you felt she needed at the time, done the best you could given the circumstances, and then you see her sitting there, telling you that all she ever wanted was a place to stay that she knew was hers, someone to love and be loved by, one person she could trust to stand by her — even though you've heard it all before, you begin to think how simple it all is, or you wonder why you didn't think of it. It's such a fresh and frank perspective. You can't hide behind the agency protocol or the lack of time. You have to seriously question your commitment because all these kids are really saying is, Give us a chance. You begin to understand that the agencies have got to change.

Because somehow, according to her [the young girl
speaking at the conference] and to many of them, we
simply weren't picking up the signals. If it doesn't
change, neither we nor they are going to get any satisfaction. I could be wrong, but I really believe we both want
the same thing.[12]

Most of the youths I interviewed frequently spoke of suicidal thoughts or past attempts as casually as they spoke of
running away. The question of whether or not to take that path
of escape is just one of the battles they face en route to adulthood. Psychiatrists typically prescribe medication to deal with
the depression that precipitated the suicidal attempt, or "nego-
tiate" contracts often based on superficial assessments, or
attempt to deal in other ways with the youths' problems without ever acknowledging the root causes that led them to consider suicide a justifiable — or the only — response. People
who feel as helpless as a ricocheting pinball can hardly be
faulted for considering death as a way of escape when all else
has failed. This, at least, is in their power.

As leaders in the Network travel into different regions, taking with them the accumulated thoughts of youths across the
country, the response for many is a sense of utter relief:
"Someone understands me." Members of the Network do not
need to deal in therapeutic cliches that have long since lost their
healing power. Their lives, lived simply and straightforwardly,
are models of possibility, opening for many the view to a way to
reshape their own lives. And with the vision, however dimly it
is perceived, comes the empathetic support that lends it sub-
stance.

If all of this sounds too simplistic, consider the example of a
young woman from Winnipeg. She had recently attended a
Network conference in Toronto, where she met and was
befriended by a number of youths from the Network. Two days
later, needing urgently to talk with someone, she called one of
the people she had met. It was two in the morning, and the
friend didn't get the message until awaking about six hours

later. Unable to reach the girl in Winnipeg, she phoned the National Youth in Care Network office in Ottawa. The staff were in Washington attending a conference. When word reached them at their Washington hotel, they put out an all-points bulletin to agency representatives and friends in Manitoba explaining that they feared the girl might be suicidal (she had a history of previous attempts). That evening, when she was finally found and told the story of the alarm that was set off across two countries in response to her call, she was distressed but happy that her pleas for assistance had been heeded. When it was discovered why she had been so upset — one of her close friends had committed suicide by jumping off a bridge just hours before she called — the Network flew her to Ottawa from Winnipeg to spend a week among people who cared, her peers.

She did not commit suicide. She made some solid friends. She was able to cope. She also made an interesting comment. She had not phoned her worker or psychiatrist because she wasn't sure she could trust their reaction. She wasn't sure she could trust them, period. In the past, they had responded to her suicidal pleas for help by locking her up, medicating her into a pliable state and waiting until the crisis had passed. Nothing had changed. None of the situations that led to her attempts had altered. But now she knew she had an alternative bulwark that would support her through such crises.

What she found in the Network was a community of people who had suffered or were suffering similar life experiences, people who understood her. And in that she found strength. It is this unconditional caring and instantaneous understanding that characterize the youth in the Network and explain its growth. This Network will become a place of refuge for young people whom adults have been unable to reach, replacing the family they never had.

The primary goal of the Network is to chronicle, and inform the child welfare systems and the general public about, the issues that matter to them. Two closely related issues of central importance are education and training for independence.

The Pape Adolescent Resource Centre — known also as PARC — is a unique model program established in 1986 in Toronto to serve youths from the three Metro Toronto Children's Aid Societies who are preparing to get off the streets or to leave the Society and strike out on their own. It is one of the few programs intimately connected with the youth empowerment movement and addresses itself to issues youth in care raise. It is also philosophically in line with the Network's aims to emancipate the youths who come into its programs, giving them responsibility and enabling them gradually to become self-determining adults. The method by which this is accomplished at PARC is in keeping with the notion that, given the chance and the proper instruction, young people prefer to work out their own salvation. With some it doesn't work: some come in too late, or they may simply want to remain powerless, a condition usually observed among those who have depended on the system longest. But for many others it effectively provokes change in their lives.

PARC serves only those youths whom they assess can stand a reasonable chance of succeeding in a highly individualized but structured environment meant to teach basic independence skills. To implement this, youths and adults work in groups, on conference presentations, on their individual goals, dealing always delicately but honestly with the frail egos of damaged, abused, afraid, vulnerable, and often functionally illiterate clients.

PARC operates out of an old house in the east end of Toronto. Dinners are eaten communally, and the menus are chosen and prepared by the youths in the program. Even something so simple as preparing a meal becomes a learning experience that years in foster or other forms of residential homes had never taught them. Some youths do not know how or where to buy food, how to budget for it or to cook it. Everything had been done for them. It is only as they are approaching 18, the age when they will officially and abruptly be cut off from the child welfare system and sent out into the world, that they begin to appreciate the need for these and other simple life skills. The problems they encounter are manifold. An integrated system such as PARC's is one of the few programs capable of responding comprehensively to their desperate needs.

Fay Martin, the dynamic social worker behind this pilot project, reports:

> In the first year of service, we noted that a high proportion of our clients had severe educational disadvantages. Some read and wrote at a grade two to four level, even though they were enrolled or had graduated from basic-level high school courses. Others were technically literate but were unable to express themselves orally or in writing, and were impaired in their ability to problem solve. Still another group were academically competent at the high school level but lacked the organizational self-disciplinary skills to be successful at post-secondary education or employment.[13]

In other words, the child welfare agencies that were responsible for them had failed to equip them with the life skills fundamental to success in our society. In an Ohio study, cited by Raychaba, the researchers concluded:

> The overall educational attainment of children in out-of-home care is dismal. Over half the children are performing below grade level in both reading and mathematics. . . . Given that these are children in the care of the state, it might be supposed that a serious effort would be taken to provide compensatory educational services to a group of children who are failing badly at school. This is not happening. . . . The out-of-home care system is intended to give children who have typically come from troubled families a chance to develop to the limits of their ability. This does not appear to be happening in the area of children's education.[14]

On the basis of this appraisal of educational deficits common among children in care, one would expect to find many remedial programs such as PARC. Unfortunately it is an exception. For most apprehended children, given the impermanence of their residence and the frequent changes in personnel and friends that plague their life, and their alienation and utter dependence on the system, school or education is one of their least important priorities. It has rarely been associated with pleasure and is not seen as necessary — until they are suddenly faced with the real world and the limited opportunities that now exist for them.

Speaking about children in care in a paper entitled "The Hidden Unemployables," Gary Corbett documents the obstacles to success that this population faces. He observes that while the unemployment rate for youth nationally runs at about 17 percent (itself quite high), the rate of a sample of teenage crown wards in Winnipeg was between 70 and 80 percent. Concerned that the Winnipeg study might present an anomaly, he contacted agencies across the country, only to discover that this figure, within a few percentage points, was relevant to all crown wards in all agencies.[15] This is the population PARC is dealing with. This is the population being created by the child welfare system that we believe is caring.

The Network has called for changes in policy that include an after-care resource person, simplified access to funding for those who want to continue their education, support services such as PARC or one of the handful of similar organizations across the country, information exchanges to keep young people abreast of what services a particular city offers, and a host of other services not currently part of the post-care experience. In one of their reports, they sum up cogently and concisely the range and nature of the problems to be addressed:

> Ex-child welfare youth, as a group, possess a unique predisposition to post-care difficulty, distress, a lack of support, and possibly even homelessness. . . . The National Youth in Care Network believes that youth leaving care of child welfare authorities are currently threatened by the multiple specters of poverty, tran-

siency, loneliness, emotional mental health problems, and homelessness to a far greater extent than most young people. In light of these concerns the National Youth in Care Network makes a number of recommendations:

That children and youth be deemed a top priority in Canada. That the care of children by the State should be conceived in terms of nurturance and support as opposed to protection. That empowerment of such youth be recognized and implemented in the child welfare system. This is best done by sharing the decision-making process. Youth must become involved in the design, implementation, operation and evaluation of the services which affect their lives. Empowerment supersedes paternalistic structures and should be encouraged by the system.

That preparation for independence be vastly improved and include on-going in-care and after-care support systems which take account of the psycho-social transitional needs of adolescents. This will require increased funds, and radical restructuring of present programs and initiatives.

That child welfare become more outcome-oriented with an emphasis on quality control.

The tree is judged by its fruits; the system must be judged by its end products. If the vast majority of adolescents leaving the system are incapable of normal life in society, then the system, no matter how well it seems to be working according to other criteria, is simply *not* working.

In addition to this quoted report, the Youth in Care Network has set out at great length a number of recommendations on other aspects of the in-care and post-care experience. They have commented on Native services, single mothers, the need for preventive services, the need for funding and resources for local Youth in Care Networks, sexual abuse allegations in homes, and treatment of sexual abuse victims, and have formed a number of clearly thought out strategies to be discussed and considered by policy designers at provincial and federal levels. These recommendations are an example of the ability of these youths, once removed from the oppressive paternalism of the system, to observe and comment upon, and initiate change within, the system of which they are the ultimate recipients. It is imperative that we listen.

8

PROGRAMS THAT WORK

I wasn't even interested in the school. I just wanted to use it to get out of jail. I'd been in Barton Street [Hamilton municipal jail] for three weeks on a remand, and one of the guys there told me about this school which would take me and if they did, I might be able to persuade the judge not to send me to reform school. I needed something. I had a record, long as your arm, as they say — B&E, car theft — fuck, I loved cars, stole 20 of them at least and got caught for most, crazy really — drugs, lots of drugs, but no violence. I'd been kicked out of countless schools. I'd been on probation, in foster homes, group homes, detention centres, training school. I was even in Guelph Reformatory for three months. Now that's a hell of a place for a kid to be. Name it, I'd done it, and I'd been there.

Home was hell. I had been on my own since I was 13, and I was 19 or so then. I had grade 10 — got that in training school — and yet I wasn't stupid. Give me a different background and you would have seen a different person, I think, but at the time that was my way of doing things. That was all I knew.

Anyway, I get one of the counsellors there to tell the school that I'm really interested and I want to be assessed. And they come down and they do an assessment and I tell them everything they want to hear — I'm not stupid, and I'm already aware of their program, so they go away and come back and tell me I'm okay for the school, but they can't make any recommendations to the court unless I'm at the school, which for me is a Catch-22: to get in I have to get out of jail, and to get out of jail, I have to get in the school.

So I'm sitting there trying to work this one out and by chance a friend of mine had returned to the city and he hears that I'm inside waiting for remand, no money for bail — most friends had long ago given up on getting me out 'cause I didn't show for trial — and he gets me out and I rush up to the school and meet this guy Anderson. He was great. He knew that I was lying about how much I wanted to be there. He knew that I was trying to manipulate myself into the program and get out of going to jail and he knew that I knew that he knew and neither of us said anything about it. We just went on as if every-thing I said was true.

To make a long story short, I got in. I go for my pre-sentence report and my lawyer tells the judge what every petty criminal's lawyer tells the judge since the begin-ning of justice, about how I've seen the error of my ways and he throws in the school and I'm working part-time and he's just got to give me a chance, and he does. Per-fect, everything working out as planned.

I was back on the street, and back and forth in the program, back and forth on drugs, not much different than before, but I liked the place and the people and I was learning something. After a while, it becomes pretty clear that they — the tutors — can see through the bull-shit, and you've got these other young guys all around you, each of them with their own weird background — mainly druggies in those days — but you have to answer to them because you're responsible for some part of the group's knowledge base. If you screw up, everyone suf-fers, that kind of thing.

It's an interesting process, but I'm still my old care-free delinquent self, constrained by court orders and these people who seemed to see right through me but who did nothing to change me. No threats, no therapies or behaviour-mod programs, nothing like that. They were there and if you wanted to learn you had to do it yourself. That was so interesting, because you had the feeling — I know it wasn't just me who felt it — that the tutors there knew you inside in some way better perhaps than you knew yourself — and yet you didn't feel they disliked you or judged you. In fact you felt they really liked you, despite the fact that they could see into you, and that was an interesting new experience for me. I didn't know quite what to make of it.

One time I was at home, hadn't been to school for three weeks, stoned out of my mind, and I hear a knock on the door and it's this guy Len, one of the tutors, a med student, and he says, "Hey, good to see you. Can you see me?" He could see I was stoned at the time. And he says they were worried about me and wondered if I was okay. And he said that no one was mad and if I wanted to come back he could drive me or he could meet me the next day. Nothing is said about judge's orders or drugs or anything, just, we were thinking about you and why don't you drop by.

After he left, I'm thinking about him coming over and thinking about his passion. He loves recorders. He has hundreds of albums and scores of recorders, all different kinds, and he would teach anyone who wanted to learn how to play. Now recorders, especially the kind of music he played on them, interested me about as much as a cold bath, but his enthusiasm, his passion, kind of tweaked my interest. I began fooling around with one and before you know it I'm thinking that I should learn to read music, and a number of other guys at the school are getting into it so we have little sessions and I'm trying to play Jethro Tull on these mousy little recorders. I went on to learn to play the flute, which I still play in baroque ensembles, believe it or not.

The reason I bring this up is that this guy and I connected and a lot of others there connected with someone else who had little things that they loved, really loved doing and sharing with anyone. If you liked it, great; if not, so what, they still had their love. So anyway, somehow I connected with this guy Anderson and a lot of others there and I just kept going and the kind of things I was learning began to interest me more than my previous way of doing things, just sort of crept up on me, and within a year, maybe two, I no longer have the details, I was completely committed to a way of life that two years earlier was incomprehensible to me. Now you have to remember, at this time I'm basically hard-core delinquent with a borderline psychopathic personality; at least you could have made a case for it as no doubt many of my workers had done, but at the same time I was reading and thinking about things that were both new and convincing at some level.

Some latent tendencies began mixing with the dominant tendencies to the point where I could no longer tell whether I was a saint or a criminal or both, which led me to study Jean Genet, the French poet-criminal-saint — I was reading a lot then and trying to learn to write — which led to the French writers of the early twentieth century, which led to the American expatriates, which led to D.H. Lawrence, which led to paganism, which led indirectly to the peripatetic life of the fifteenth-century abbot and scholar Abelard, of Abelard and Heloise fame, whom I spent my entire undergraduate years trying to fathom.

The rest, as they say, is history. I don't know when it happened, but a process began there which even today, 20 years later, continues to have influence on the way I view the world. I still have friends from that period, all of whom will tell you in their idiosyncratic fashion a story similar to mine. I think we're still trying to figure it out and wondering during those dark nights of the soul, which seem to come more frequently as you get older, what would have happened if Cool School had never been. What in God's name would we have become?

Graduate of Cool School, now a private-school teacher.

Jim Anderson stood in the foyer of St. Michael's rectory. As a young medical student in training, and a practising Catholic, Anderson had planned to go to the Third World in the tradition of Albert Schweitzer and use his expertise where it was most needed. He had come to this office directly behind the towering St. Michael's Cathedral to speak with Sister Rita about it. But as he looked out the window on that long-ago day, Sister Rita's voice rang in his ears like the bells of St. Michael's at noon. "Everyone wants to go somewhere else and help. Maybe it's more exotic, I don't know. But look around you. Take a good close look at these streets. The Third World doesn't have a monopoly on the sick, the blind, and the lame. Just as many here would be thankful you came."

Years later, as a professor of anatomy at McMaster University's innovative medical centre, and a practising psychiatrist specializing in adolescent problems, Anderson could be found almost any day or night of the week at one of the city's drug clinics or out on the streets listening to stories of the good dope and bad times of struggling adolescents. During the late 1960s he became a central member of the Le Dain Commission, established by the federal government and directed to explore, explain, and seek solutions to the substance-abuse "epidemic".

Anderson was a man of broad tastes. He appreciated the works of Hermann Hesse and Isak Dinesen, fine wine, Gregorian chant, computers (long before they became popular), Carl Jung, anthropology and archaeology, the Latin mass, Teilhard de Chardin, bad puns, and most areas of medical science. He had a whimsical sense of humour. But above all, he was dedicated far beyond the call of duty and seemed to learn as much from the adolescents he worked with as he taught them. According to students and colleagues who worked closely with him, he was a gifted, complex, and inspiring teacher.

During the late sixties Anderson conceived of a school that would appeal to the alienated, frequently stoned street kids of Hamilton, Ontario. Most of them were without jobs, skills, or a future. He gathered around him an eclectic assortment of medical students, musicians, and anyone willing to share their interests with these youths in a structured setting. "Cool" was the operative word of the day, and in short time Anderson had an alternative school, the name of which spread even before the band of minstrels and teachers had a chance to formulate their goals.

Cool School was set up in an old house on the grounds of Hamilton's Chedoke Hospital. It was linked loosely with the hospital's child and adolescent programs. Its mandate initially was to serve youths who would not or could not conform to the more highly structured setting of the typical school. The youths who came to it were referred by community-based guidance counsellors, child protection agencies, probation officers, psychiatric clinicians, worried parents, or other youths. It catered primarily to underachieving drug abusers who were often delinquent in other ways as well. Cool School was a last-resort facility for those who had failed elsewhere.

Students worked in groups that were loosely structured and had lots of latitude to evolve, with just enough of a baseline to form a distinct starting point. The teaching method relied upon discreet tutorial direction, and peer group discussions and evaluations. Individual and group goals were shared openly. It was an eclectic environment: a loose coalition of outcast individuals working within a controlled but flexible framework.

Only two rules brooked absolutely no exceptions. First, no drugs on the premises; second, don't hurt anybody. Books and furniture were scrounged. Each student became responsible for his or her stated, or developing, "area of expertise." It cost nothing to attend. Many of the youths who enrolled were temporary or full-term wards of the state. Some were on welfare or working part-time. Some were the walking wounded of middle- and upper-class broken families. If they needed assistance, anyone from the secretary to the spouses and lovers of the staff would work with them informally. Most of the students could read or write at basic levels.

Some of the students were dismal failures. Some exhibited previously untapped genius. Trying to match individual strengths and weaknesses among the students in each group, fuelling the need for and awareness of their interdependence, was an important part of the group leader's function. All performance measures were geared towards fostering greater independence and interdependence among their peers, rather than dependence upon other authority figures. In this community-building milieu, youths who had been labelled schizophrenic, delinquent, psychopathic, and paranoid became instead maverick scholars. They uncovered abilities they never knew they had and formulated more and increasingly richer goals.

Along the way, various youths picked up skills and knowledge in music, sports, ecology, photography, wilderness adventure, astronomy, math, computers, and literature. Most importantly, they gained self-knowledge. Of the youths in this program, many of whom had been labelled disturbed and channelled into vocational schools, over 70 percent graduated to university or went on to lead self-determined, productive lives. Doctors, lawyers, professors, journalists, nurses, a botanist, a microbiologist, teachers, an anthropologist, dancers, architects — and one sheep herder — are listed among the graduates of Cool School.

Many of the youths who graduated from this alternative community consider their tenure there *the* changing point, the milestone in their life. The question is, how did it happen? And why there? What did they do right? Stan Eaman, a Hamilton psychiatrist who referred a number of youths to Cool School, attributes its success to the stability amidst the chaos and to the long-term commitment of the staff.

Ted Ridley, cofounder with Jim Anderson, former journalist, award-winning photographer, and the longest full-time tutor/group leader, becomes characteristically ambiguous when journalists and students probe the reasons for the success of the program, now entering its twentieth year. He, too, credits the dedication of the staff; many have now been there for more than a decade. He suggests that a rigorous screening process weeds out the potential failures before they get there. Cool School, he says, won't work for everyone. So who does it work for, and how does he choose the potential successes? He's not sure. Everyone queried on the subject seems to imply a certain subjectivity about just what makes some people fit that forum. But I would submit that the personal-judgment element is itself a crucial, if not totally defined, key to the school's success. It is precisely this — having the time and freedom to deal closely, over the long term and on a one-to-one basis with young people (something most social workers lamentably lack, as earlier documented) — it is this *personal* relationship, full of intangibles, that contributes to the success of the program.

In its heydey, Cool School worked for many underachieving, rebellious adolescents. Over the years its admission requirements have changed to meet the needs of the changing adolescent community. Currently it provides services using the same "formula" (and with the same success rate) to youths with severe learning disabilities, most notably dyslexics. Because they have difficulty reading, dyslexics are shunted into remedial classes and vocational schools. By the time they reach adolescence they are defined by and embarrassed by their illiteracy. Since their condition often cannot be accurately diagnosed or treated, society views them as second-class citizens. And they come to believe they are indeed incompetent.

Cool School assesses their level of competence and trains from there. They "name" the disability and suggest various paths towards a cure. This frank recognition of the impairment, without the denigration that usually accompanies such labelling, brings a sense of relief. The potential cure, if it can be called such, is based on the belief that given the proper environment, the dyslexic *can* learn, and that beyond the superficial, often aggravated dysfunctional social behaviours lies an individual with something worth expressing. In an adaptable learning environment using group dynamics, peer pressure, individual guidance, and realistic goal setting, dyslexics become confident of possibilities they had never before considered. They are accepted by others, and they begin to accept themselves as their range of competence increases. They are shown that the limits society sets are not absolute, and they are taught ways to transcend them. In short, they are empowered.

Cool School worked initially because of the charismatic leadership and unorthodox vision of Jim Anderson. But its continuing success without him at the helm (he has since retired) suggests a formula that, while difficult to pinpoint, deserves careful study.

Cool School, PARC, McMan Youth Centre, Central Toronto Youth Services, the National Youth in Care Network, and a few other isolated programs within the child protection system share elements that maximize success. They screen their staff well, perform rigorous assessments on applicants to their programs, run a semi-democratic rather than autocratic organization, share responsibilities among staff, and exhibit a deep and abiding respect for children wanting to break out of their psychological imprisonment. They do not offer token solutions, nor do they promise what they can't deliver. They encourage what strengths they see rather than harp on the obvious weaknesses. They empower rather than criticize. They provide stability, structure, and vision. Yet in all this, they make individuals responsible for their own behaviour at whatever level they can bear. They create a space, that is to say, for progress and achievement to be visible, so that small successes can lead to greater success.

In almost every case, the adolescents I have spoken with mentioned a mentor who brought them to the point where they could envision something beyond the limited horizon of their experience. Cool School, PARC, McMan, and the other programs all provide a guide or confidant to the youths who come to them. It is required of the staff that they commit themselves to the program for at least two years, thus providing the youths with a potential bonding partner. Since most youths who come into such programs are mistrustful of adults, the mentoring process is taken very seriously.

At Central Toronto Youth Services, this concept is considered so vital that even if a child is moved through other agencies or foster homes, they attempt to maintain the link between a child and one person who will remain with the child no matter where he or she is in the system. Often they are able to match former prostitutes with street kids, or reformed criminals with juvenile delinquents, so the young person has both permanence and true empathy in the one-to-one relationship. Cool School graduates all speak of some*one* within the program as being responsible for their ability to transform themselves and take advantage of the program. Once that bonding occurred and the tools of the program could be used independently, the future was opened to them.

The model that Cool School represents is grounded in the idea of a democratic community. It is commonplace that youth in care, who feel cut off from their friends, parents, and community, and who no longer speak the language of the mainstream, are viewed as loners, and feel alone. Yet this is not inherent in them as individuals; when given the opportunity to act in concert with others, in a sense to build a common language, they demonstrate the ability to do so. It is in fact what they long for. One of the spinoffs of creating a successful community-building process is that it is also fulfilling to the *staff*; thus burnout is less common and there is more likelihood of bonding between staff and the young people in their care. Clearly, such an environment generates mutually satisfactory relationships.

This combination of elements rarely occurs in traditional systems. The inflexibility of bureaucratic regulators, the paternalism and one-way communication of many child-worker relationships, unfounded assumptions about the abilities and needs of youth in care, and imperfect theoretical models applied via the medical model of servicing, which leads to an inappropriate pyramidal model for implementing agency servicing — the most knowledgeable practitioner at the top and the least knowledgeable at the bottom — all combine to act against innovation, democracy, shared responsibility, and mentoring. Youths are not empowered; their increasingly strenuous attempts to break out of the pre-set moulds as they grow older and more vocal are met with matching, increasingly stifling strictures. The adolescent remains powerless, or rather, incapable of measured exercise of power or self-assertion, but more prone to volatile shows of power in unpredictable and unproductive outbursts.

There is a curious similarity to the structure of programs that don't work. They are top-heavy, for one thing: those who spend the most amount of time with the child or adolescent have the least authority to influence his life circumstances. According to Dr. Mark Krueger, a radical American psychologist, there are historic reasons for this. Krueger has suggested that when social services for abandoned or neglected children became a separate field of professional endeavour at the beginning of this century, most workers were strongly influenced by the monumental discoveries of Freud and the psychoanalytic concept of therapy: find the "cause" of the "disease" and "erase" or cure it. (It would be several decades before more holistic approaches focussing instead on growth and fulfilment would appear.) Social workers relied upon medically trained psychiatrists to develop treatment models for their allegedly mentally disturbed clients. Adolescents perceived as mentally unfit became the exclusive domain of psychiatrists (or social workers trained by them) engaged in laborious and time-consuming studies of the mind and the painful unravelling of unconscious and repressed conflicts.

After World War II, psychologists and social workers began to assume a more prominent role in directing and conducting the residential treatment plan. But like the psychiatrists they were replacing, they were severely limited by their small number and their large caseloads. Care givers, such as the growing number of foster parents, house parents in cottage-type residential centres, and youth workers, vastly outnumbered the academically trained professional staff in the child protection industry, yet they remained underutilized in the treatment programs and stigmatized by low pay and minimal authority. This top-heavy model persists to this day, putting an effective stranglehold on the talents of the "lowly" front-line worker.

Against all common sense, people still think that somehow a disturbed child can get better from only the one hour a month he spends with the elite psychiatrist rather than from the myriad *daily* contacts with the foster parents or live-in counsellors at the residential centre. Psychiatrists and psychologists rely heavily on "objective" testing procedures such as the Rorschach test, MMPI, and case histories received at second hand. A lot gets lost between the conveniently computer-readable little squares that need to be checked off. In addition, psychiatrists and psychologists do not necessarily have a good knowledge of practical solutions to problems or of the availability of appropriate services. Their training is primarily clinical, and they rely upon less sophisticated community-based services to deal with the youths who don't require their specific training. Thus the psychiatrist is often ineffective and unnecessary, while his handmaiden, the social worker, frequently spends a great deal of her time serving as a mere broker between the community services, such as emergency shelters or employment training programs, and the young client. Until the front-line child care workers receive the support and recognition that the higher level of professionals receive, child care services will limp along at third-rate quality.

Over the past two decades the child care worker movement in the United States has been gaining recognition for its radical restructuring of the adolescent treatment model. Mark

Krueger and his associates have mapped out alternative structures and functions of treatment programs that effectively
remove clinical staff from their positions of power and substitute instead a "team treatment approach," which places
authority and responsibility equitably in the hands of all team
members, including group home and residential staff and foster parents. The mutually helpful and sharing relationship
between all levels of staff tends to reduce, if not eliminate,
much of the archaic character of the current approach.

What Krueger and others are attempting to forge is a system
that can best use the talents and knowledge of all people working with youth. Wherever they have been able to implement
this model, surprising changes have taken place. Staff tend to
stay longer and youth tend to respond. The reason is simple:
theirs is a variation of the model represented by places like
Cool School. For example, under the current practice the tendency for foster parents or group home parents — the primary
care givers — is to limit their interactions to a custodial function. Krueger's model, though, has these workers fully
involved in the therapeutic process. Increased pay scales reflect
their change in status. Feeling that their input is valued, these
workers do not burn out so quickly, can spread their positive
influence wider in the structure, and can achieve greater levels
of excellence. With their increased job satisfaction, they
remain working, which means that the youths have a chance to
bond with them, to learn to trust them while developing their
own levels of competence. In short, what Krueger's model does
is maximize the contributions of everyone involved in the caring process.

To successfully propagate programs such as Cool School or
Krueger's project requires more than the brief analysis that I
have given here, but such analysis is essential. Only programs
that foster a sense of community, and that recognize achievement when it occurs, will be successful. Why should a child
shine if his gains are not celebrated anyway?

Given the level of restructuring required to adopt Krueger's
model, it will not be easy to displace traditional entrenched

models of service delivery. But it *is* possible. With new legislation that sets out explicitly the rights of youth in care, with the active involvement and dissemination of information on youth in care through the Network, and given the frankly acknowledged ineffectiveness of many programs within the child protection and treatment industries, there may be more willingness today than in the past to consider initiating large-scale changes. At the very least, there will be greater toleration of the isolated pockets within the child welfare field where unorthodox workers' successes continue to challenge older paradigms and put more effective ones in their place.

9

...AND IF THEY DON'T?

*The strange and foreign is not interesting — only
the deeply personal and familiar.*
John Steinbeck, *East of Eden*

Society's failure to deal with troubled youth is nowhere more clearly observed than on the streets of North America's major cities, where tens of thousands of desperate youths wander aimlessly. In 1986, *Maclean*'s magazine commented on the ever-increasing number of street people:

> No one knows how many thousands of people trudge
> from hostels to soup kitchens on Canada's streets. But
> church and social workers agree that their composition
> is changing. Only a decade ago most were men in their
> 40's and 50's, "winos" whose presence was taken for
> granted as a fixture of urban life. But the new homeless
> ... include large numbers of children and young peo-
> ple.[1]

Who are they? Why are they there?

Most of us, walking down Hastings Street just east of Vancouver's Gastown, or St. Denis in Montreal, or Toronto's Yonge Street Strip, easily avoid the "flaunting little whores" and shabby young men who cross our path. We read about them in the mainstream press and listen with half an ear to their stories in revealing broadcast documentaries. But we don't really know them, and most of us don't want to. They cease to be sons and daughters in our minds. Instead they are transformed into underworld figures, predatory teenage gangs, shadowy performers of illicit trades whose acts are as sensational as their young age.

But they are hard to ignore. In every major North American city homeless street youths have become a dominant presence. Ranging in age from 13 to 25, coming from black, white, Native, and newly arrived immigrant populations, predominantly from the ranks of the poor and the lower-middle classes, they sell their bodies and their souls for survival on the capricious, often dangerous streets. A growing number, contrary to popular opinion, come from the middle and upper classes, the fallout of a lifestyle that their two-income parents loved more than they loved their children. The street is no respecter of class. Rich or poor, youths are there to escape hopeless situations. They run from abusive homes, either their own or their surrogate, state-appointed families.

A Calgary study found that of 405 runaway children, over one-half had run from child welfare placements, that is from foster or residential homes. This, the researchers concluded, suggests "that our alternate provisions for young victims of family breakdown, neglect and abuse fall short in meeting their needs." The responses of the young people interviewed indicated that the provisions available to them were perceived as "control" rather than "care".[2] Street workers in other major cities responding to the Calgary study speculate that as many as 60 percent of street kids they encounter are on the run from child welfare placements. Whatever the final tally, certain characteristics are common among those who take to the street: a feeling of transience, an inability to form relationships, confusion and depression, insecurity, dismal economic prospects, and abysmally low levels of education. These are also the characteristics common to the graduate of the child protection system.

As these adolescents take to the streets, absorbing its values and enduring exploitation by both veterans of the street and the straight society that has pushed them aside, they build up a resentment that later taints their relationships with other people.

After interviewing homeless children in Vancouver, Montreal, and Toronto, Dr. Ellen Morgan concluded that more than 70 percent of homeless people are clinically depressed to the point where they are indistinguishable from their counterparts in psychiatric settings.[3] Furthermore, many of them are violent. Virtually any street worker can report dozens of horror stories about the violence committed and threatened by the children and adolescents they encounter, often against the kids themselves as their rage is inverted and vented against their own bodies. Only a small percentage of incidents are reported publicly.

In earlier chapters I noted the research that suggested that continual drift through the system tended to create psychopathically disturbed young people. Studies of the prison population have confirmed that most inmates have histories of childhood abuse or neglect and are unable to form meaningful relationships. The most horrific examples of what such maltreatment can lead to comes to light in the phenomenon of serial killers. During the last decade, 36 multiple murderers have been captured and confessed to killing, collectively, hundreds of victims. Twenty-three — nearly two-thirds — of these vicious murderers had been long-term wards of the state, passing from a very early age onward from foster home to group home to institution. At worst, the state system seems in some cases almost to have created them. At best, it failed completely to alter their path or heal them during their tenure inside the system.

Some of these multiple murderers argue that their acts were the only experiences that gave them a sense of unadulterated pleasure. This is what Charles Manson said when convicted of murdering Sharon Tate. During the highly publicized court proceedings, he told of his life in various institutions before he drifted onto the streets, where he met his "girls"; he accused society of "doing this to me and my girls." In a way, he was right. Manson and men like him were removed from their homes or were abandoned, and were processed by a system that sincerely intended to identify their needs and help them. But help never arrived. We do, of course, hold Manson responsible for acts he committed when he was an adult and in possession of his faculties, but how do we judge what happened, or failed to happen, during the many years he was in care and seen by a score of psychiatrists and social workers and foster parents? Manson is but one gruesome example — an extreme example — of how inappropriate or ineffective the child welfare system can be. But there are other, closely similar cases. Is this the price society pays for its failure?

"Son of Sam" Berkowitz, who raped, murdered, and mutilated many women over an extended time, gave a revealing analysis. Berkowitz was an adopted illegitimate child who was shunted off to foster homes and institutions throughout his life. He had this to say:

> People feel a certain eeriness about me, something cold, inhuman, monsterus [sic]. . . . When I look at all the prisoners in King's County Hospital I cannot help but feel sorry for them. They're like lost souls, in and out of institutions all of their lives; little hope, no family, no friends. I think people only want peace and comfort in life but apparently few know how to find it. It seems like the only saviour these patients have is thorazine [an antidepressant drug used to pacify psychotic patients].

The last entry scrawled in the diary, between a picture of a sad face and a doodle, are the words "HELP ME."[4]

Berkowitz's analysis of what drove him to commit unfathomable acts is not far removed from the pattern seen in the lives of many in child welfare: alone, passed from foster home to institution, depressed or enraged. Recall Dr. Elliot Barker's saying, "Show me someone who has been in 10 foster homes and I'll show you a psychopath," or Dr. Paul Steinhauer's idea of creating psychopaths "without even trying." It may not be conceivable that we have in fact designed a breeding ground for the psychological disorders of adolescents, but it seems to have already occurred in the United States and it is a concern that mainstream Canadian researchers are beginning to address.

This is the price society pays for its failure. "The street" might, indeed, be seen almost as part of the failing system, as an intermediate stage or "institution" to which lonely, unskilled, and angry youths gravitate after moving successively through the previous stages of state care and which they leave only to enter still other state institutions, hostels or prisons, food banks, missions, or psychiatric hospitals. Looking at it this way makes it impossible to avoid feeling some responsibility for what goes on on "the street" and to see it rather as part of a larger whole that needs serious attention.

It is important to understand the street milieu, to understand what it is that many of the graduates of foster and group homes prefer above our solutions. Most arrive with severely limited options, flat broke, no possessions, few skills and little useful education, often literally lost and unfamiliar with their surroundings. They place themselves at the mercy of more experienced street people who will ultimately help them overcome their ignorance or force them into a convenient niche in the hierarchy of the street. Within days they gravitate to one of the many street subcultures: to the ranks of the teenage (male and female) prostitutes with diamond earrings and snakeskin boots, to the even more marginal caste of transvestites who draw the spite of almost everyone, to the green-haired skinheads with pins through their noses, to the petty criminals, bikers, and roaming gangs of boys and girls dressed deceptively in prep clothes or dark leather. They stand in the glare of the neon lights, with little money in their pockets, eyeing the surrounding predators. They remain essentially alone, but the need to be there, the need for, if nothing else, physical proximity to others who share their predicament, compels them to stay.

The terms "homeless" or "runaway" apply usually to persons under the age of 16. It is generally felt, and seems to be implied in some legislation, that a young person should be allowed to voluntarily withdraw from parental or state control at that age. However, under the federal Young Offenders Act, persons up to the age of 18 can be apprehended and returned to their "legal abode". Both federal and provincial legislation seeks to balance society's concern for the individual rights of young people and their families with the state's interest in their protection. But the ambiguity and controversy surrounding the interpretation of such wording as "substantial risk" and "a child in need of protection" (Section 40 of the Young Offenders Act) make police feel incompetent to deal with such children. To the youths, impervious to the intent of the various acts designed to protect and control them, life on the streets is hell, especially for the young prostitutes.

Some prostitutes develop an uneasy relationship with the police, whom they see as their protectors from the capricious violence they are prey to by virtue of their profession. Others find themselves continually harassed, fined, and insensitively treated by the "pigs". The johns, or tricks, cruise the street casually, barely glancing in the direction of the kids they are about to pay for a blow job or some other titillating sexual escapade. But the right glance, indistinguishable to the uninitiated, leads to a flurry of negotiations, soon after which a young girl, maybe the john's neighbour's daughter, is in the car in a nearby back alley, or a parking lot, or less frequently the prostitute's room, performing her tricks with a "familiar stranger".

It is disturbing that the brutal life of a young girl or boy on the street is supported by men who could easily be respectable fathers, probably with children of the same age. The girls say that stockbrokers, accountants, teachers, police, professors, journalists, and politicians are all part of their clientele; they pay a good price. They also say that it doesn't matter to them who they get into the car with, so long as it's safe. Judgments on this point are often inaccurate.

Red, the name given to her on the street because of her flaming red hair and her tendency to blush when she tells of bizarre sexual practices, decided at 13 that she had had enough of foster care. Since then she has worked the streets in Vancouver and Toronto, and though she makes more money in Toronto, she likes Vancouver better and would like to go back there someday.

Someday? A vague notion in her mind. She doesn't give much thought to the future. She thinks the future broke down for her when she was nine years old and then came completely apart every week for two years after that, while her father sexually abused her. When she was just over 10 she informed her brother. They weren't close — "he had his own problems" — but she had no one else to confide in. About two weeks later her brother, sympathetically, she thought, started asking her what it was like, but then came into the room when she was changing and started "doing things to me just like my dad." This went on regularly for about three months. One day, expecting her brother to come into her room again (she didn't feel there was anything she could do against her violent father), she put a pair of scissors under her pillow. She stabbed him in the arm and thinks she would have killed him if his screams hadn't brought her father to the door.

> I was so mad, I think I would have got my dad if he tried anything, but he just burst into the room, saw the blood and [my brother] kind of curled up by the window, looked at me, and without saying nothin' pulled my brother out of the room. My brother had to go to the hospital and get stitches and shots. My dad wouldn't go with him. After that my brother never talked to me, just snarled, and my dad didn't say nothin'.
>
> Oh yeah, my mom, she don't do nothin' around the place ever. She's nothin' to me or my old man. I don't know why they stay together. They don't like us and they don't like each other. I don't think I talked to her about anything since I was, I dunno, seven, maybe eight.
>
> After the thing with my brother, I asked a counsellor at school if I could talk with someone about my prob-

lems. A little bit after that I got to be put in a foster
home, which was okay in a way 'cause I didn't have to
put up with my house anymore, but it wasn't any good
there. I don't mean the foster people were bad, it just
wasn't, you know, like your own place. I ran away twice,
and the second time they said that I should be in a group
home, 'cause [the foster parents] couldn't figure me out
or something. I met some kids there who had been living
here [on the street]. One of them said that she was going
to go back. She said she had friends and that she could
get a place to stay and I said that I wanted to go with her.
So we came here. I was 13 then.

"Here" is Toronto, home to an estimated 12,000 street kids.
Home here was initially a subway shelter (the friends the other
girl had spoken of had moved to parts unknown), then a series
of temporary shelters in the city, and finally a run-down,
roach-infested apartment with a constantly shifting population of runaways, one of whom eventually got her into prostitution.

I listened to her, because she was nice to me. She was
three years older than me [16] and had been on the
streets for seven months. She started making money
after about five months but she couldn't bring herself to
do it all the time, you know, get in with some guy and let
them do stuff to you. It was awful at first, she said, but
then you get used to it and you can just forget about it. I
knew what she meant there. That's how it was with my
dad. And she had money too. Everybody else was stealing the stuff from the bakeries or the delivery trucks, or
rolling some drunk, that kind of stuff, but they never
had money or anything. That's why we had to stay in
this shit place. But [my friend] had money, enough of it
anyway, and by the time I got to know her, she was ready
to move to a better place with other girls who were doing
it and she said that I could come too. I said sure, and

then I started too and I began to make money. I was
lucky, I guess.

In many ways Red's story is typical of street kids. Abuse,
sexual and otherwise by their families, the escape, the failed
meeting with social-service providers, the lack of skills, which
ultimately will cement their bond to the street, and the almost
inevitable slide into prostitution — these are the realities
behind most of the growing number of kids on the streets. And
in this particular rendition, although it sounds perverse to the
ears of most middle-class North Americans, Red may indeed
have been lucky, as she herself says.

Lucky?

On the streets, among the scarred young victims of abusive
parents and the failing child protection system, Red luckily
escaped the scenario that awaits most girls like her: submission
to a pimp, one of the fixtures of street life. The 1984 Badgley
Commission on Sexual Offences Against Children and Youths
had this to say about pimps:

> The relationship between young prostitutes and pimps
> encompasses one of the most severe forms of abuse of
> children and youth, sexual or otherwise, that currently
> occurs in Canadian society. The relationship is based on
> two forms of ruthless exploitation: psychological and
> economic. The pimp exploits her low self-esteem, her
> feelings of helplessness, her loneliness on the street, and
> her need for love and protection. These weaknesses are
> the fetters with which the pimp binds the girl to him and
> keeps her on the street. Economically, pimps exploit
> prostitutes by drawing them into a form of virtual slave
> labour, or at least into a relationship in which one party,
> the pimp, provides a service whose value is vastly out-
> weighed by the amount the other party, the prostitute, is
> required to pay for it. The cost to the prostitute of work-
> ing for a pimp goes far beyond the earning that she gives
> him; it amounts to the girl's forfeiture of her future.

When a girl like Red enters the street, the pimp or one of his girls will recruit her into his "stable". The pimp will vie for the girl's attention at a bus stop or a particular hangout that is known to attract desperate girls who are hitting the street for the first time. In a well-practised routine, he will sympathize with her plight and offer his friendship, his protection, and the possibility of love, without of course mentioning his ulterior plan. He will, in effect, complete the girl's escape from the world of adults who failed her, through a subtle manipulation of her fears and inarticulate desires. But he will exact a price for filling that need and hope for love. Generally within a few weeks, he will introduce her to the underside of the world that he has conned her into. He will speak of their mutual need for money and the easy manner in which this financial problem can be resolved. He or one of his girls will accompany her on the street the first couple of times. She soon learns the ropes. Often, rather than admit to prostituting for the man she hopes loves her, she will rationalize what she is doing as necessary for their mutual success. Even after the inequity of the situation is apparent, she will try to harmonize her former hopes and the obvious ignominy of what she is doing by reference to some supposed long-term plan.

But in the real world, where her illusion has no currency, she will become in the minds of her pimp, her johns, and eventually the general public just a whore. She will thereafter be treated as such and in time come to think of herself in exactly the same terms. During those moments when the mask is removed and she perceives her situation as it really is, she will note that she has few friends, that those who once knew her now condemn her. She will realize that the only people who understand her are her "friends" on the street. She will have it reaffirmed by the larger community she services that she is not a valued member, and that in this consumer society, she too is only a commodity. Her lack of skill and references puts conventional jobs out of reach. She will in effect be locked into the life of the street until someone breaks into her world with a vision worth striving for. To escape the bleak realities of her life, she will retreat into drugs, deviance, or death by suicide, a common occurrence among street people.

Half of the boys and two-thirds of the girls I talked to admitted that they had contracted a sexually transmitted disease. Dr. Clyde Cave at the Toronto Hospital for Sick Children studied 50 young prostitutes, boys and girls, and found that 70 percent of them were carrying sexually transmitted diseases. The most frequently reported was gonorrhea — over one-third had been infected with it at least once. Next was syphilis. The HIV virus associated with AIDS was found in nine people in the study. However, given the high degree of communicability of this disease, and given that almost 40 percent of the prostitutes admitted that they had continued working the streets after they had been infected with a less virulent disease, AIDS will likely continue to spread among prostitutes as well as among their clients. One male prostitute, after being told that he had tested HIV-positive, responded, "Okay, I've had it. Now I'm going out and shaft the world who gave it to me." AIDS is also spread equally among boys and girls through intravenous drug use and promiscuous bisexual relationships. Very few street people practise safe sex, since that would mean thinking about the precariousness of their lives on the streets, and thinking about that is the one thing that most of them refrain from. It would be too depressing.

Drug and alcohol abuse are almost universal. At present, nearly all prostitutes in Canadian cities would consider themselves, or be classified as, addicted. Crack is becoming a major problem, with crack houses operating in Toronto, Montreal, and Vancouver. With the increase in crack use, police expect an increase in mugging, break and entering, random and unmotivated violence, and sexual assaults.

For the girls on the street, violence is just part of the sordid business. By far the worst abuse they suffer is at the hands of their pimps. As reported by the Badgley Commission, and confirmed by street outreach workers and by the girls themselves, whipping and beating is common, along with other sadistic forms of intimidation such as branding, being thrown from moving cars, or mutilation. Frequently they are humiliated in the presence of other prostitutes and pimps to illustrate the pimp's control and impress rivals, or to show how macho he is and to serve as a warning to other girls not to get out of line. Profound psychological abuse is a daily occurrence.

As for their tricks, every time a prostitute steps into a car it is an act with an uncertain outcome. Tricks are, for the most part, "normal" middle-class men out for a little "harmless", unconventional activity. They are the primary "support system" for this youthful commodity. It is difficult to understand what motivates men who go to young prostitutes or how they can separate the wounded innocence of pubescent girls on the street from their feelings towards their own daughters. Some women have suggested that the prevalence of father-daughter incest, just now coming to be recognized by society, might be even higher without the accessibility of child prostitutes. If that is so, there may be profound questions on sexuality that we have hardly acknowledged or begun to address. But even if this is true, it is still difficult to understand how the respectable middle-class men who constitute the prostitute's clientele can sanction the frightening context in which the prostitute who serves them lives. Perhaps the pimp who brutally regulates the disordered lives of his girls is simply a kind of landlord, or broker, whose role is to keep his stable of girls in line and ready for the use of "straight" men.

But the trick is not always so harmless. Every girl has a story to tell about harm suffered at the hands of a sadistic trick. Angel (her street name) is a 19-year-old hooker whose ambition is to become classy enough to get off the streets, because, she says, call girls at the hotels only have to work with businessmen, who are far more predictable. She adds, "My father is in business, you know," as if that explains something about her "career" choice. On the street, though, she has to deal with her own fears of unpredictable men and the fears of younger kids who look to her as both a veteran hooker and a bit of a mother figure.

I always try to look out for the little ones. They got it

real bad. They get here and they don't know shit about
anything. So I tell 'em what to expect and what not to do
and what to look out for, that kind of thing. Then when
it happens, and it's gotta happen sometime, they know
they can come to me and I'll help them out. I'll even take
time off, you know, like lose a lot of money to help them
straighten out.

This woman, a mixture of the cool professional and the
sympathetic mother figure, grew to maturity on the streets of
half a dozen Canadian cities. Two years after she had left her
fourth group home, she started working the streets. She was
14. She quickly turned to prostitution, initially with a pimp,
but after the roughhousing and lousy pay she struck out on
her own. Not long after setting up in Toronto she got in a car,
was driven to a familiar parking lot, and while performing
fellatio was stabbed three times in the back. She was tied up,
put in the trunk of the car, and driven by her trick to a
deserted place, where he raped her repeatedly, stabbed her
three more times, and left her for dead. Miraculously, she got
loose, crawled to a nearby highway, and was taken to a hospital. Two months after her assault she was back on the street.
Showing some of her scars with a perverse pride, she says,
"See that? I can survive anything. You got to be tough to
make it, and I'm gonna make it."

She says she thinks she's weathered the worst part of "the
life" and that she can now take anything that comes along. "I
can look at you and know if I should go anywhere near you.
It's a sixth sense I've got now." It is this knowledge she tries to
impart to the new girls who arrive on the street, although she
believes you have to experience the savage unpredictability of
attack before you can really make up your mind about the
street. As a result of the assault, she has steadily moved on
towards the hotel/convention trade. "I mean, if you like it and
you want the money, you can really be someone. They really
appreciate someone who's got class, and they'll pay for it."

Some of the kids on the street will get out within a few years through some happy circumstance and go on to live productive lives. Many more will remain in the rut that kept them on the street, and even though they may become tired and too old for the street, their lack of skills and preparation for entrance into the larger community will leave them living lives of quiet desperation in solitary rooms, getting by on welfare or low-paying menial jobs. Still others will become criminals, and others will become the bag ladies and derelicts of the future. Like the child welfare system, the street, it seems, is indifferent to the fate of its former residents.

The failure of the state to solve abused children's problems is magnified when these children have their own children. The seriousness of teen pregnancies generally, and on the street specifically, is reflected in the fact that young adolescents face a greater risk of death from pregnancy and its complications. Compared to women in their early twenties, the death rate from complications is 35 percent higher for 15-to-19-year-old mothers and 60 percent higher for adolescents 14 and under. And despite the talk of support, the suicide rate among adolescent pregnant youths is seven times that of non-pregnant teens.

Over half of teenage pregnancies end up aborted, legally or illegally. Of those who do have the baby, most prefer to keep them and will try everything in their power to stop state agencies from apprehending the child and giving it up for adoption. That is certainly admirable, but with their history of abuse, their lack of skills, and their marginal subsistence on welfare, it is almost inevitable that their children in turn will end up in the child protection system.

So why is the street, with its vagaries, abuses, and general squalor, so alluring to these children? Only the tiniest fraction of youths who hit the streets ever choose to return to their original home or their foster home or institution. Difficult as it is to accept, is not their repudiation of the system indicative of some very fundamental flaws in our way of helping young girls and boys? That anyone could find prostitution preferable to what their family or the straight surrogate system offers is so stunning that mainstream society has been unable to seriously address the questions that need answering.

Very few services exist to meet the needs of these street kids. Since they operate on reverse-time — sleeping during the day and hitting the street at night — they do not have access to the conventional social services. Since they are accustomed to immediate gratification, they reject the slow bureaucratic programs that attempt to reach them. Most of them, with their distrust of authority and their history of moving through the social-service system, will find it extremely difficult to approach any authority within the straight world.

For those few who do try to make it back, the road is long and difficult. They are ghettoized into menial, meaningless, low-paying occupations. They are exploited and harangued by snooping landlords. They struggle alone to balance budgets, coordinate daycare, find new romantic relationships, all without having the social skills most of us take for granted. Even if minimally successful in merging with the straight world, they carry with them, like shell-shocked veterans of war, the strange mannerisms and defensive postures that will forever set them slightly apart. It is no wonder there is such a high rate of recidivism. It is, rather, a wonder that any at all *do* manage to find a relatively normal, productive social life.

In 1985 the Canadian Child Welfare Association voiced its concern with the mental health of 16-to-24-year-olds and the dearth of programs to help them until they are truly integrated into society.

> Aside from coping with the usual developmental problems of adolescence, they are burdened with additional stresses resulting from their chaotic life experiences. Additionally, 16-24 years is an age of relatively high risk for the onset of major mental health illness and it is essential that such illnesses be identified and treated early. Yet, this age group experiences great difficulty in obtaining continuity of mental health services. Even in

locations where children's services do exist, adult mental health programs are reluctant to admit hard-to-manage young people, while the children's programs shy away from involvement with near adults. It is nothing short of tragic that community-based programs which meet young people's critical need for continuity of mental health care do not exist.[5]

This is tragic, because for all their mistrust and condemnation of the world around them, they do need assistance when they want to return. According to Fred Mathews, a Toronto community psychologist,

Social workers, police, and our education system had an inadvertent role to play in the process of an adolescent's entrance into and entrenchment in prostitution. Intimidating and bureaucratic structures of practice, restrictive service mandates, inadequate professional preparation and complicity with the status quo notions of order and morality all contributed separately or in some combination to an adolescent's decision to try prostitution or to remain in it as an income-producing activity. A true awareness of the lived reality and the pressing problems faced by these young people was clouded by a great deal of moralistic and bureaucratic baggage.[6]

It almost seems that the only people who are successful in reaching this young population are those who have one foot in both worlds, the conventional child saving system and the outcast subculture. The programs that succeed are non-judgmental, open at all hours, and crisis-management-oriented. Among the most successful of the street-level services is Father Joseph Ritter's Covenant House, a project started in New York about a decade ago to deal with the growing population of street people in that city. The message and the methods seemed to work, and Covenant House is now established as well in Puerto Rico, Texas, and Toronto, where inner-city youth and homeless people meet in the violent sub-culture of the streets.

It requires very special, highly dedicated workers to reach street kids. They must be available at any hour of the day or night and must act more as surrogate parents than casework-ers, the opposite of the typical shirt-and-tie, nine-to-five, paper-shuffling bureaucrats who fill most social-work agen-cies. Adolescents generally, and adolescents on the street even more so, are hard to process through a uniform system. They don't lead organized lives. In addition, social workers on the whole do not enjoy working with adolescents; they prefer very young children in whom they can more easily see tangible improvements and changes in behaviour; that is inherently and immediately rewarding. Working with elderly people is also preferred, since for the most part the older person is appointment-oriented and psychologically more willing to accept assistance.

But adolescents almost by definition are rebellious, testing constantly, loud, aggressive, and against everything — or so it would seem — that the social worker believes in. They fre-quently miss appointments, are hard to keep track of, are hard to get welfare for (they usually have no fixed address or none that they want to give to the worker, and no official I.D.), are emotionally demanding and in a constant state of exaggerated crisis. Mathews suggests that adolescents take more time and energy per person to achieve measurable results than any other sector of the population that comes into state welfare agencies. Thus, energy and resources are shifted to where more quantifi-able results can be achieved, and the adolescent population is left with the short end of the stick just as they reach the thresh-old of adulthood. It is clear that once they reach this crucial stage, their families and society find it as difficult to enter their world as they do to enter ours.

One could think of the street as a battleground in which the warfare is more subtle, more quietly continuous than open gang fighting, or "swarming", though the anger does sometimes erupt in that form. This is a war of attrition, in which an overwhelming, smug, closed society leans on those in the sub-culture whom it does not understand and cannot accept.

The number of older children entering the system is grow-ing. If we don't do something now out of compassion, then in another decade or so we will have to do something out of necessity, to placate a generation of displaced and angry adults who will care as little about us as we have cared about them.

EPILOGUE

Writing this book has been something of a catharsis.

It wasn't meant to be. I had intended to write from an objective, journalistic standpoint, without regard to my own past. Giving a voice to disenfranchised children seemed to me a noble and necessary cause. But as I listened to the stories told by children and adolescents across Canada I was drawn reluctantly into my own past, a past which I had spent years vigorously trying to escape.

Like many of the children and adolescents in this story, I too passed through family courts, foster care, group and detention homes, training and reform schools. While interviewing for this book, I remembered, in a way that I had not for a long time, the brutality and mindlessness I encountered in these child protection centres. I remember enormous steel doors clanging behind me, staff laughing at my inadequacies, school children taunting me for being a foster child, foster parents beating me, and myself retreating further and further into a private, distorted world. I remember, too, some of those who tried to help me, for there were kind people about, but at some point — I can't say precisely when — the child in me that was innocent but unloved, was wounded, beaten back emotionally and physically, and another persona arose in its place. For many years that child in me was dead. I too ended up on the streets.

Against all chance, when I was seventeen I met Jim, a man who recognized and resurrected the child in me. He demonstrated by his actions that I was loved unconditionally, not if I would do certain things or be a certain way, but just because I was a human being, because I was *me*. I couldn't help but respond. I had been pushed into vocational schools, and reminded time and time again that I was "no good and going nowhere." Until I met him I believed that. I cannot now recall clearly how many layers were wiped away in that encounter. But I remember, as if it were yesterday, feeling for the first time in my life that I was free to explore the world and embrace it according to my abilities. Immediately, or so it seems to me now, I set upon a course to forget the past and lunge into the future. But the past does not let go that easily.

It took another decade to take control of my future. I dwelt for two years in a monastery, returned to university, then travelled around the world before finally returning to Canada. I was — at the time I thought it was by choice — an outsider, arrogant, iconoclastic. One of the options for outsiders, as Colin Wilson long ago pointed out, is art. So I turned to writing. It wasn't easy. I was twenty-four, and though I had gone to university I only barely knew how to write. It took a few years to learn. It was a few more years still before I began writing about children and returning, sideways as it were, to the past I had spent so many years escaping.

I could almost feel it viscerally when my own childhood memories came crowding back during the writing of this book. Very early in the research I was reading about Richard Cardinal and the message he scrawled on the bathroom mirror in his own blood: "Please, help me". Somewhere from deep in the past which I had tried to obliterate, I recalled when I had reached out to someone, crying, and pleading in precisely those agonized words: please, help me. I was lucky: someone did. No one helped Cardinal. He committed suicide. I had often thought of doing the same thing.

At that moment the book changed; it became intensely personal. I still intended to say nothing directly about my personal experiences. I felt my sympathy would inform the writing, keep it on track, without my having to say anything about my past, publically. But this conspiracy of silence is precisely what one needs to fight against. The stigma attached to children in care by society dictates that they keep silent, as if they themselves were to blame for the nightmare that constitutes childhood in care. One has to be discreet for one's family's sake, to avoid embarrassing them. One has to keep silent for one's own sake — it does no good to re-open old wounds, they say, one has to get on with life. But the old wounds, if not dealt with properly, have profound psychological repercussions. They have to be understood and confronted before they can be truly healed. I have no reason now to be silent. I am surrounded by a community of friends, a lovely wife and child, and relatives who have helped me in more ways than I can say. I am both fortunate and grateful.

Writing this book assisted that cleansing of my past. The voices of the children and adolescents recorded in these pages are my voice, in the sense that the experiences they suffered twenty years ago, and still suffer today, are the same as I suffered; loneliness, confusion, emotional traumas, self doubt, even self-hatred.

My elation on learning of a Youth in Care Network stemmed from my own experience of having found along the way people who had gone through the same institutional experience as I, and were successfully coming to terms with it. We became models to each other of a better world, a world filled with imminent possibility. It was not as formalized as the youth in care network, nor was it in any way political, but it was healing. We wondered then, as these kids wonder now, how does one legislate affection?

I imagine that many of us who have gone through foster care or reform school and come out the other end intact have much to say to those who are now going through the system. Unfortunately, one of the things that is taken away by the institutions into which children are thrown is the ability to trust another person, to become open and vulnerable. Thus, the very thing they need most, namely love and kindness, is the very thing they are unable to attain. If this book has any effect at all, perhaps it will ignite a desire among graduates of the system to help, however they are able. Who else really understands what it was like? Who else could hear, really hear, what these children are saying? Neither we nor they have anything to be ashamed of, although I know that shame and guilt over our past are the residue of our shared experience.

I hope this book conveys some of the pain that thousands of children in care feel and that in some small way it helps to relieve it. The last thing they need after a childhood devoid of love is to continue to live as if they deserve now to be punished for having been unwanted. They must come to know clearly that the adults upon whom they depended *knowingly* betrayed them, that they themselves are not to blame.

It is the adults who designed the programs that were forced upon them who must find the courage to admit that the system fails in many instances. It is the adults who must find the compassion and wisdom to redress the balance of power in favour of the children. We, as adults must find what is best for them by listening to what they say to us long before they end up in public inquiries. And no matter how they say it, I think they want what I once so desperately needed: somebody, anybody, to love them.

ENDNOTES

PREFACE

1 Wodarski, John, address to social workers and other professionals at a conference, University of Chicago, July 1988.

CHAPTER 1

1 John ——— , aged 27, in an interview with the author, Hamilton, 1988.
2 Bevan, Jack, cited in Ontario Children's Aid Society, *The Future of Foster Care: Towards a Redesign in 89* (Toronto, 1988), p. 8.
3 Rosenblum, Barbara, cited in *The Future of Foster Care*, p. 7.
4 Besherav, Douglas, *Protecting Children from Abuse and Neglect* (Springfield, Ill.: Charles C. Thomas, 1988), p. 83.
5 *The Future of Foster Care*, p. 177.
6 *The Future of Foster Care*, p. 8. The authors note that the report is to be followed by two further phases outlining long-term goals and issues facing service providers and funders. However, they also note that their conclusions are drawn from and represent only this specific population and should not be taken as representative of the population of foster children generally.
7 Health and Welfare Canada, *Basic Facts on Social Security Programs* (Ottawa, 1987), p. 6.
8 Cited in Thomlinson, Prof. R.E., *Case Management Review*, a report prepared for the Northwest Region, Dept. of Social Services and Community Health, Alberta, (1984), p. 169.
9 Steinhauer, Paul, "How to Succeed in the Business of Creating a Psychopath Without Even Trying" (unpublished manuscript, 1979), pp. 3-4.

CHAPTER 2

1 Cherry———, 24 years old, in conversation with the author, Toronto, 1988.
2 Gaylin, Willard, *Doing Good: The Limits of Benevolence* (Toronto: Random House, 1987) p. 23.
3 Bowlby, John, "Separation Anxiety," *International Journal of Psycho-Analysis* Vol. 41, pp. 89-113.
4 Bowlby, John, *Attachment and Loss*, volume 1 (New York: Basic Books, 1969), p. xii.
5 Martin, Freda, cited in the Toronto *Globe and Mail*, March 19, 1988.
6 Freud, Anna; Goldstein, Joseph; and Solnit, Albert, *Beyond the Best*

Interests of the Child (New York: Macmillan, 1973), p. 37. Probably the single most influential book on intervention.

7 Fraiberg, Selma, "Psychopathology, Human Values and Parenting Roles," *Journal of the Society for the Prevention of Cruelty to Children* Vol. 6, No. 9 (February 1985): p 3.

8 Bowlby, John, "Psychoanalytic Study of the Child" Vol. 15 (1966): pp. 49, 52.

9 Freud, Goldstein, and Solnit, *Beyond the Best Interests*, p. 24.

10 Steinhauer, p. 5.

11 Gaylin, *Doing Good: The Limits of Benevolence*, p. 23.

CHAPTER 3

1 *In the Best Interests of the Child*, A report by the National Council of Welfare on the Child Welfare System in Canada (Ottawa, 1979), p. 17.

2 Argles, Paul, *The Duration and Stability of Child Placement: A Predictive Study*. (Quebec Social Service Ministry, 1983), pp. 1-3, 11-14.

3 *Child In Care Review*, "A Report to the Minister of Social Services for Saskatchewan" (1988), pp. 11-19.

4 Rosenberg, Monica, in Vancouver *Sun*, August 23, 1989.

5 A couple who requested anonymity, in conversation with the author, Toronto, July 1989.

6 Foster parents quoted in *The Future of Foster Care*, p. 130.

7 Dawson, Ross, "Report on Abuse in Foster Care", prepared for Ministry of Community and Social Services (Toronto, 1988).

8 Ontario Children's Aid Society, *The Future of Foster Care*, pp. 60-61.

9 Kevin, 17 years, in conversation with the author, Edmonton, August 1989.

10 Toronto *Globe and Mail*, May 16, 1989.

11 Silverman, Peter, *Who Speaks for the Children?* 1st edition (Toronto: McClelland and Stewart, 1978), p. 79.

12 Silverman, *Who Speaks for the Children?* (2nd Edition, 1988), p. 51.

13 Silverman, p. 93.

14 Rose, Sheldon and Edelson, Jeffrey, *Social Work Practice with Children and Adolescents* (Springfield, Ill.: Charles C. Thomas, 1987), p. 8.

15 A male social worker now working in administration in Toronto. Like many within child welfare, he agreed to speak only on the condition that he remain anonymous.

16 Parent, 36 years old, in conversation with the author, Vancouver, July 1989.

17 Parent, in conversation with the author, Toronto, November 1988.

18 Social worker to the author, Edmonton, June 1989.

19 John Pine, former social worker, in conversation with the author, Vancouver, July 1989.

20 Silverman, *Who Speaks for the Children?* 1978, p. 143.

21 Corbett, Gary, *The Hidden Unemployables*, paper delivered at the University of Calgary, January 21, 1985, p. 6.

22 *Permanency Planning*. Handbook prepared by the Ontario Ministry of Social and Community Services (Toronto, 1977), p. 4.

CHAPTER 4

1 Foucault, Michel, *Madness and Civilization: A History of Insanity in the Age of Reason* (New York: Vintage Books, 1973), p. 17.
2 Rooke, Patricia, *Discarding the Asylum* (Vancouver: UBC Press, 1983), p. 244.
3 Jones, Andrew, and Rutman, Leonard, *In the Children's Aid* (Toronto: U. of T. Press, 1981), pp. 135, 139.
4 Rooke, *Asylum*, p. 284.
5 Rooke, *Asylum*, p. 367.
6 Lithwick, N. H., cited in *Poverty in Canada*, "A Report of the Special Senate Committee on Poverty" (Ottawa, 1972), p. 33.
7 *Poverty in Canada*, p. 24.
8 *Poverty in Canada*, p. 37.
9 *Poverty in Canada*, p. 46.
10 *Poverty in Canada*, p. 55.

CHAPTER 5

1 Hepworth, Philip, "Child Neglect and Abuse," in Levitt, Ken, and Wharf, Brian, eds., *The Challenge of Child Welfare* (Vancouver: University of British Columbia Press, 1985), pp. 32-39.
2 Callahan, Marilyn, "Public Apathy and Government Parsimony: A Review of Child Welfare in Canada," in Levitt and Wharf, *The Challenge of Child Welfare*, p. 18.
3 Kahn, A., and Kamerman, S., *Not for the Poor Alone* (Philadelphia Temple U. Press, 1975), p. 172.
4 Child and Family Service Act, 1984, Ontario, Section 37(2)(a)-(h).
5 Personal communication with the author, Toronto, 1988.
6 Cruikshank, David, "Child Abuse and Neglect Prevention," in Levitt and Wharf, *The Challenge of Child Welfare*, p. 184.

CHAPTER 6

1 *Child Welfare Programs*, policy handbook, Alberta Ministry of Community and Social Services (1983), p. 135.
2 Hepworth, Philip, *Foster Care and Adoption in Canada* (Canadian Council on Social Development, 1980), p. 120. See also McKenzie, Brad, and Hudson, Pete, "Native Children in Care," in Levitt and Wharf, *The Challenge of Child Welfare*, pp. 125-135.

CHAPTER 7

1 Dan, thirty years of age, in conversation with the author, Edmonton, 1989.

2 Personal communication with the author, May 1988.

3 Gerry Manfield, NAYPIC staffperson. Personal communication with the author, May 1988.

4 It should be noted here that Troy Rypstra, another young man who galvanized the project during its formative years, is held in equal regard by the current membership. Indeed, Marleen, Caroline, Tina, Marc, Kevan, Alix, Carleen, Lisa, Jason, Twilla, and many others who have been instrumental in developing the Network, will know how much they are appreciated. I in no way want to single out one or another of the founding members; however, I know the story of Dallas better than I know the others' and am therefore more comfortable telling that story.

5 Quoted in personal papers from the National Youth in Care Network archives.

6 I have paraphrased the message Dallas and his colleagues conveyed at various conferences. Culled from the National Youth in Care Network archives.

7 Interview, Toronto, August 1988.

8 Cited in Stein, Mike, and Carey, Kate, *Leaving Care* (New York: Blackwell, 1986), p. 5.

9 Interview with John Meston, July 1988.

10 Raychaba, Brian, *To Be on Our Own with No Direction from Home* (manuscript, National Youth in Care Network, 1988), p. 3.

11 Raychaba, *To Be on Our Own*, p. 51.

12 Interview with social worker Sherry Slater, at a conference in Toronto attended by social workers, child care workers, and members of the federal and provincial governments considering the question of "drift" in care. It was one of many recent conferences where youth in care were invited to present their thoughts on the issues. September 1988.

13 Martin, Fay, "Literacy Program Proposal", a report prepared for the Ontario Ministry of Community and Social Services, 1987, pp. 1-2.

14 Raychaba, *To Be on Our Own*, p. 53.

15 Corbett, Gary, "The Hidden Unemployables," cited in Raychaba, *To Be on Our Own*, p. 31.

CHAPTER 9

1 *Maclean's* magazine, January 13, 1986.

2 Symposium on Street Youth, Covenant House, Toronto, 1988.

3 Dr. Ellen Morgan, speaking at the Covenant House conference cited above.

4 Leyton, Elliott, citing Berkowitz's prison diary, in *Hunting Humans* (Toronto: McClelland and Stewart, 1986), pp. 160–65.

5 *Mental Health and Adolescence*, report to the Ontario Ministry of Community and Social Services on mental health in young adults (Ottawa) 1986, p. 90.

6 Mathews, Frederick, *Familiar Strangers* (Toronto: Central Toronto Youth Services, 1987), p. 3.

BIBLIOGRAPHY

Admittance Restricted: The Child as Citizen in Canada. Ottawa: Canadian Council on Children and Youth, 1978.

Albert, S. James. *Children and the State.* Proceedings of a conference at the School of Social Work, Carleton University, Ottawa, April 16-18, 1978.

Aldridge, M., and Cautley, P. "The Importance of Worker Availability in the Functioning of New Foster Homes." *Journal of the Child Welfare League of America*, Vol. 54, No. 3 (May 1987).

Argyles, Paul. *The Duration and Stability of Child Placement: A Predictive Study.* Quebec: Social Service Ministry, 1983.

Bala, N. *Review of the Ontario Child Abuse Register.* A thesis written for McGill University. Kingston: Queen's University Press, 1987.

Besharov, Douglas, *Protecting Children from Abuse and Neglect: Policy and Practice.* Springfield, Ill.: Charles C. Thomas, 1988.

Bowlby, John. "Grief and Mourning in Infancy and Early Childhood." *Psychoanalytic Study of the Child*, Vol. 15 (1966).

———. *Attachment and Loss.* Volume 1. New York: Basic Books, 1969.

Canadian Child Welfare Association. *Proceedings of the National Consultation on Adolescent Prostitution*, 1987.

Canadian Child Welfare Association: Past ... Present ... Future, A Review. Toronto, 1988.

Child in Care Review. Saskatchewan: Minister of Social Services, 1988.

Corbett, Gary. *The Hidden Unemployables.* Address at the University of Calgary, 1985.

Cox, M. *Foster Care: Current Issues, Policies and Practices.* Norwood, NJ: Ablex Publishing, 1985.

Dawson, Ross. "Report on Abuse in Foster Care." Prepared for Ontario Ministry of Community and Social Services. Toronto, 1988.

Denholm, Carey, ed. *Professional Child and Youth Care: The Canadian Perspective.* Vancouver: U.B.C. Press, 1983.

Florence, Hollis. *Casework: A Psychosocial Therapy.* New York: Random House, 1964.

Foucault, Michel. *Madness and Civilization: A History of Insanity in the Age of Reason.* New York: Vintage, 1973.

Freud, Anna, Goldstein, Joseph, and Solnit, Albert. *Beyond the Best Interests of the Child.* New York: Macmillan, 1973.

The Future of Foster Care: Towards a Redesign in '89. Toronto: Ontario Children's Aid Society, 1988.

Gaylin, Willard, ed. *Doing Good: The Limits of Benevolence.* Toronto: Random House, 1987.

George, Vic, and Wilding, Paul. *Ideology and Social Welfare.* London: Routledge and Kegan Paul, 1976.

Hepworth, Philip. *Foster Care and Adoption in Canada.* Ottawa: Canadian Council on Social Development, 1980.

———. "Trends and Comparisons in Canadian Child Welfare Services." Paper presented at the First Conference on Provincial Social Welfare Policy, Calgary, 1982.

Heywood, Jean. *Children in Care: The Development of the Service for the Deprived Child.* London: Routledge and Kegan Paul, 1978.

Horejsi, Charles. *Foster Family Care: A Handbook for Social Workers, Allied Professionals and Concerned Citizens.* Springfield, Ill.: Charles C. Thomas, 1979.

Johnston, Patrick. *Native Children and the Child Welfare System.* Toronto: Canadian Council on Social Development, 1983.

Jones, Andrew, and Rutman, Leonard. *In the Children's Aid: J.J. Kelso and Child Welfare in Ontario.* Toronto: U. of T. Press, 1981.

Kendrick, Martyn. *Anatomy of a Nightmare: The Failure of Society in Dealing with Child Sexual Abuse.* Toronto: Macmillan, 1988.

Krueger, Mark. *Careless to Caring for Troubled Youth: A Caregiver's Inside View of the Youth of the Care System.* Minneapolis: Tail Publishing, 1983.

The Legal Framework for Ending Foster Care Drift. Washington, D.C.: American Bar Association, 1983.

Levitt, Ken, and Wharf, Brian, eds. *The Challenge of Child Welfare.* Vancouver: U.B.C. Press, 1985.

Leyton, Elliott. *The Myth of Delinquency: An Anatomy of Juvenile Nihilism.* Toronto: McClelland and Stewart, 1979.

———. *Hunting Humans: The Rise of the Modern Multiple Murderer.* Toronto: McClelland and Stewart, 1986.

McConville, M., and James, J. *Proceedings of the First Annual Symposium of Street Youth.* Toronto: Covenant House, 1986.

Macneil, John. *Preparation for Independence: Planning and Learning for Independent Living.* Toronto: Ministry of Community and Social Services, 1984.

Martin, Fay. "Literacy Program Proposal." Prepared for the Ontario Ministry of Community and Social Services, 1987.

Mason, W.A. "Determinants of Social Behaviour in Young Chimpanzees." In *Behaviour of Nonhuman Primates: Modern Research Trends*, edited by Schrier, A., Harlow, H., and Stollnitz, F. New York: Academic Press, 1965.

Mathews, Frederick. *Familiar Strangers: A Study of Adolescent Prostitution*. Toronto: Central Toronto Youth Services, 1987.

National Council of Welfare. *In the Best Interests of the Child*. Ottawa, 1979.

———. *Poor Kids*. Ottawa, 1975.

Page, Raissa, and Clark, G. *Who Cares?: Young People in Care Speak Out*. England: National Children's Bureau, 1983.

Poverty in Canada: Highlights from the Report of the Special Senate Committee on Poverty. Ottawa, 1971.

Preparation for Independence. Prepared for the Ontario Ministry of Social Services, 1984.

Raychaba, Brian. "To Be on Our Own with No Direction from Home." from Manuscript. National Youth in Care Network, Ottawa, 1988.

Rooke, Patricia. *Discarding the Asylum*. Vancouver: U.B.C. Press, 1983.

Rose, Sheldon, and Edelson, Jeffrey. *Social Work in Practice with Children and Adolescents*. Springfield, Ill.: Charles C. Thomas, 1987.

Silverman, Peter. *Who Speaks for the Children?*, First edition. Toronto: McClelland and Stewart, 1978. Second edition, 1988.

Stein, Mike, and Carey, Kate. *Leaving Care*. New York: Blackwell, 1986.

Steinhauer, Paul, Dr. *How to Succeed in the Business of Creating Psychopaths Without Really Trying*. Unpublished version of article, April 1979.

Thomlinson, R.J. *Case Management Review*. Prepared for the Northwest Region, Department of Social Services and Community Health, Alberta, 1984.

Three Decades of Change: The Evolution of Residential Care and Community Alternatives in Children's Services. Toronto: Ministry of Community and Social Services, Policy Development, 1983.

Tiffin, Susan. *In Whose Best Interest? Child Welfare Reform in the Progressive Era*. Westport, Conn.: Greenwood Press, 1982.

INDEX